Priscilla Hauser's Book of Decorative Painting

Priscilla Wait Hauser

NORTH LIGHT BOOKS
Cincinnati, Ohio

A Note From Priscilla

When learning to paint, to cook, to sew or practically anything else, one needs to remember there are many "right" ways, not just one. The methods and techniques that I am presenting to you in this book are a small portion of the many techniques I have learned and developed. With practice, you will find they are easy to do and bring pleasant results.

Through more than three decades of teaching people how to paint, I have taught the old, the young, the sick and the well. My painting career has taken me to Japan, Europe, South America, Russia, Australia and hopefully in the future, Korea and Africa. Students come from as far away as Israel and Malaysia to my beautiful little studio by the sea, which is located in the pan-handle of Florida between Panama City and Destin. There we teach people not only how to paint, but to teach, if they desire. For a schedule of my seminars and locations, along with a list of my publications and videos, please write to Priscilla's Little Red Tole House, Inc., P.O. Box 521013, Tulsa, Oklahoma 74153-1013.

Priscilla Hauser's Book of Decorative Painting. Copyright © 1997 by Priscilla Wait Hauser. Manufactured in China. All rights reserved. No part of this book may be reproduced in any form or by any electronic or mechanical means including information storage and retrieval systems without permission in writing from the publisher, except by a reviewer, who may quote brief passages in a review. Published by North Light Books, an imprint of F&W Publications, Inc., 1507 Dana Avenue, Cincinnati, Ohio 45207. (800) 289-0963. First edition.

Other fine North Light Books are available from your local bookstore, art supply store or direct from the publisher.

01 00 99 98 97   5 4 3 2 1

Library of Congress Cataloging-in-Publication Data

Hauser, Priscilla Wait.
    [Book of decorative painting]
    Priscilla Hauser's book of decorative painting / by Priscilla Wait Hauser.—1st ed.
        p.   cm.
    Includes index.
    ISBN 0-89134-722-4 (alk. paper)
    1. Painting—Technique. 2. Tole painting. 3. Folk art. 4. Decorating and ornament—Plant forms. I. Title.
TT385.H35 1997
745.7′23—dc21   97-3544
                                                                              CIP

Edited by Greg Albert and Jennifer Long
Production edited by Marilyn Daiker
Designed by Chad Planner

North Light Books are available for sales promotions, premiums and fund-raising use. Special editions or book excerpts can also be created to specification. For details, contact: Special Sales Manager, F&W Publications, 1507 Dana Avenue, Cincinnati, Ohio 45207.

METRIC CONVERSION CHART		
TO CONVERT	TO	MULTIPLY BY
Inches	Centimeters	2.54
Centimeters	Inches	0.4
Feet	Centimeters	30.5
Centimeters	Feet	0.03
Yards	Meters	0.9
Meters	Yards	1.1
Sq. Inches	Sq. Centimeters	6.45
Sq. Centimeters	Sq. Inches	0.16
Sq. Feet	Sq. Meters	0.09
Sq. Meters	Sq. Feet	10.8
Sq. Yards	Sq. Meters	0.8
Sq. Meters	Sq. Yards	1.2
Pounds	Kilograms	0.45
Kilograms	Pounds	2.2
Ounces	Grams	28.4
Grams	Ounces	0.04

Dedication

My husband, Jerry
No greater love have I

Acknowledgments

I would like to thank the following individuals
for their assistance with the development of this book.

Janet Stewart	Judy Kimball
Naomi Meeks	Linda Posey
Pat Tanguay	Alta Bradberry

Walnut Hollow's David Ladd and Cindy Perrin-Gorder

Table of Contents

A handy guide to all the supplies you'll need for decorative painting in oils and acrylics, including which brushes to use and how to care for them.

Learn how to properly prepare today's most popular surfaces for your decorative painting, and how to protect and finish your projects when you're done. Also included are six easy techniques for adding beautiful decorative finishes and trims to any project.

Practice these fundamental skills—from painting basic brushstrokes to blending in both oils and acrylics—and you'll be on your way to painting beautiful, lifelike flowers in no time.

These step-by-step demonstrations will show you how to paint a variety of leaves—from simple to more complex—to accent any type of flower.

With the help of my step-by-step demonstrations and paint-along worksheets, you'll soon be painting lush, lifelike florals on everything in your home! Over a dozen flower varieties are presented, each including gorgeous project ideas—complete with patterns for you to trace—that are sure to inspire you.

Introduction

Yes, yes, yes. You *can* paint! Why? Well, if for no other reason, for the pleasure it will bring you—and it certainly will bring a great deal of that. I'm Priscilla Hauser and I've been teaching decorative painting for more than thirty years. I can honestly say that each year I continue to paint, the world of painting becomes more and more exciting to me.

It all began in 1952, when I was twelve. I had spent the night with a friend who had the most beautiful hand-painted furniture, including a rounded top trunk, covered with roses. From that moment, I was bound and determined to have furniture covered with roses.

Priscilla and Picasso

When I told my mother and father the price of these beautiful, hand-painted treasures, my mother smiled and said, "I'm sorry Priscilla, they cost too much money." However, that following Christmas, a camel back trunk was under the tree. No, it was not covered with roses. A note was attached telling me I should learn to paint roses and decorate the trunk myself. My mother even took me to see the woman at the used furniture store who had painted my friend's trunk. When I asked her if she would teach me to paint roses, she laughed, and in a rather unkind voice said, "I do not teach anyone how to do that, dear." However, in the course of the conversation, she did refer to the technique as tole painting, and a seed was planted. (Today, I know the word *tole* is French for tin, and that tole painting is only the painting or decoration of tinware, but at the time, I thought all roses painted on furniture were called tole.)

Although I had always loved to draw and paint, it seemed at first that was not to be my destiny. My parents stepped in and said, "No, we won't send you to art school. You need an insurance policy, a way to make a living." And, of course, they were right, because I would have been a flower child in art school, probably way out in left field, no telling what I would have created!

Instead, I found myself cleaning teeth in the Baylor Caruth School of Dental Hygiene. I stayed in school until the day I looked out my little apartment window and saw the love of my life, Jerry Hauser. For me, it was love at first sight, the end of the teeth-cleaning episode, the beginning of our life together and the beginning of my painting career.

Jerry and I married and moved from Dallas to Kansas City. Having always been active in YWCA activities, I sent for the local Y's brochure and to my amazement and delight, a course in tole painting was offered. I struggled through six weeks of lessons, pregnant with our first child and vomiting every day, but I made it. I did not have the money to buy a large, red sable flat brush, but my mother saw to it that I had one.

That was all it took, six lessons. Indeed, I painted roses. My first roses on a saltshaker graced our table for many years. The roses looked like horse droppings flying in lettuce leaves, but I loved that saltshaker. Today, I like to think that it is an inspiration for students everywhere as they begin to indulge themselves in one of the most beautiful and elegant art forms there is, decorative painting.

In 1962, Jerry and I moved back to my birthplace, Tulsa, Oklahoma. We now had two young children. While I loved motherhood, the call of the brush never stopped ringing in my ears. My painting continued.

Soon neighbors saw that I was transforming trash and treasures from garage sales and flea markets into wonderful home decor. They asked me if I would teach them how to paint. I decided that this might be an interesting way to make some extra money, but I knew that I could not take their money unless I had a real method of teaching them the techniques that I did. So I began to work out ways to teach my techniques, step by step, to try to make it as easy for them as possible.

Soon, so many people gathered around the Ping-Pong table in our garage that their cars blocked our neighbors' driveways. I was turned in to the Tulsa Zoning Commission for running a business in my home. A change had to be made.

I moved my studio to the back of a Sherwin-Williams paint store where I

The first Priscilla's Little Red Tole House

The second Priscilla's Little Red Tole House

happily taught classes for a couple of years. The desire for my own business raged within, and it was not long before Jerry found a little house that had been an antique store. With hard work, and the help of my students, we sanded, painted and cleaned. Soon Priscilla's Little Red Tole House was born.

Classes at The Tole House continued to grow. Money I received from classes was reinvested in inventory. I had 275 students a week and I was teaching three classes a day. My business demanded so much of me that I was exhausted, but I loved it.

In 1969, my only brother was killed in a motorcycle accident. I was devastated. He had a small insurance policy and the money was divided among the three surviving sisters. I used that money to publish my first book on dimensional glass painting. Thus, Priscilla's Publications was born.

Decorative painting was becoming increasingly popular. I felt that all people who loved this hobby should unite. In October, 1972, I asked all the teachers, shop owners and seminar students that I could think of to come to Tulsa for a meeting, and at that meeting I founded the National Society of Tole and Decorative Painters.

The early days of the Society were difficult ones, not only for me, but for all of us who struggled to make it grow. But dreams do become realities. You just have to work to make them happen, and never give up. Today, this organization has approximately thirty thousand members with chapters

Priscilla and Jerry at Priscilla's Studio by the Sea

throughout the United States, Canada, Japan, Australia, Germany and South America. It is so much fun to reminisce back through the years, and to dream of what it will be tomorrow.

In 1974, I was invited to teach a seminar in Opelika, Alabama. The seminar sponsor, a beautiful woman named Joanne Walker, took one look at me and decided I was working too hard. She invited me and my family to her beach home in the panhandle of Florida, on the Gulf of Mexico. On that Fourth of July weekend, I fell madly in love with the beautiful white sands and the aquamarine water. I could not stand to be away from it, so we purchased a little condominium on the Gulf. Twelve years later, we built Priscilla's Studio by the Sea.

In 1983, after many years of publishing my own books, I sold Priscilla's Publications, including my magazine *Priscilla Hauser's Workbook*, to the Martin/F. Weber Co. In 1987, the magazine was sold as the *Artists' Workbook* to F&W Publications and renamed *Decorative Artist's Workbook*, a bimonthly magazine that has grown out of the tradition that began in *Priscilla Hauser's Workbook*.

Also in 1983, I had the incredible honor of being asked, as the representative of the United States, along with ten artists from other countries, to paint a panel to be presented to His Royal Highness Prince Bernard of the Netherlands. At that time, the Prince was President of the Worldwide Wildlife Foundation. The paintings we created were printed in the form of greeting cards to raise money for the foundation.

This was the first and only time I had ever been invited to a palace, and as I floated out of the back seat of the car, standing under a big umbrella in the gently falling rain, I looked in amazement at the red carpet leading up the stairs to the palace door. I couldn't walk and I couldn't talk, but Jerry pinched

me and I quickly came back to my senses and climbed the steps into the palace.

When Jerry and I opened Priscilla's by the Sea, as hard as it was for me to do, I knew I had to close Priscilla's Little Red Tole House in Tulsa. In my Florida studio I continue to teach painting seminars to people that come from all over the world. These seminars are designed for beginners, as well as the more experienced decorative artists.

Decorative painting is a magnificent fine art form, full of skills and techniques that can be learned by absolutely anyone. You see it really does not take talent to paint. True talent is a God-given gift that has been bestowed upon a few, but the ability to learn has been given to all of us. Painting is for all of us who wish to be creative, to express ourselves, and to paint beautiful gifts and items for our homes, families and friends.

So follow me through this book into the magical world of decorative painting. Study the book carefully, practice the skills, and remember, "With brush in hand, my mind empties of its sorrows and the beauty in life smiles." If you keep practicing and painting, you will keep smiling!

Priscilla and His Royal Highness, Prince Bernard of the Netherlands

A Glossary of Terms

Following is a list of terms often used in the world of decorative painting. Some are common to all forms of art, others are exclusive to decorative painting. I recommend you read through this list before going any further; it always helps to know the language when finding your way around a new place.

Acrylic Extenders or Retarders— These are chemicals that can be added to or used with acrylics to help extend the time you have to work with them before they dry.

Acrylic Paint—Acrylics are a polymer emulsion, or in other words, a liquid plastic. They are water-based so they dry quickly and are thinned and cleaned up with water. They are available in tubes and bottles.

Antiquing glaze—a product available as a water-base glaze or an oil-based glaze, aplied over a sealed surface and wiped with a soft or textured rag so you can control the amount left on to give an aged look to a piece.

Applying an Anchor—To float a dark shading color, shadow or highlight over a basecoated subject.

Banding—Painting a band, stripe or trim on your project. Straight, even bands can be created by taping off the area to be banded with painters' tape. Striping can also be done with a brush.

Basecoating—To paint a piece of wood, tin or other surfaces with 2 or 3 coats of paint, before decorative painting is done, or to undercoat the actual design area. This should always be applied smoothly and evenly as possible.

Blending—The combination of two or more colors. It is usually done with a flat brush.

Blending on Palette to Soften Color— When double-loading a brush you must stroke it repeatedly in one area on the palette so that the two colors will blend together softly where they meet in the middle of the brush.

Brushstrokes—A series of strokes, such as the comma and S-stroke, which are practiced and perfected until they can be performed uniformly. These are the alphabet of decorative painting.

Clear Acrylic Spray—Used for sealing porous surfaces, but should be used only in a well-ventilated area.

Color Book Painting—Filling in a solid area between the pattern lines with one uniform color, as with a child's coloring book.

Contrast—Contrast is the key to beautiful painting. It involves sharp differences between two or more colors used on the same subject. Contrast makes your painting look alive. If you learn to paint with contrast, your work will have zip and sparkle, light and life. God has created this world with lots of contrast and in order to make our work beautiful, contrast is extremely necessary.

Crackle Medium—Many companies make a medium, which when the directions are properly followed, will give you a cracked background. I enjoy using the crackle mediums for special effects.

Decorative Painting—I define decorative painting as the painting or decoration of any surface. Under this definition come the many styles of painting found throughout the world. Decorative painting can include such surfaces as furniture, household accessories, floors, walls and even the outside of houses.

Directional Stroke Blending—To blend by stroking along the natural curves and lines of the object you are painting.

Dirty Brush—A dirty brush is a brush that has paint in it and has simply been wiped on a rag before continuing with the painting.

Double-Loading—To carry two colors side by side on a brush. Where the two colors meet, they should blend together gradually.

Floating—A technique in which the brush is filled with painting and blending medium or water on one side, and paint on the other. Used to create shadows and highlights.

Flyspecking—A technique applied by filling a toothbrush or other flyspecking tool with thin paint and spattering a fine mist of paint over the surface.

Folk Art—Folk art, varying from simple to elegant in style, is painting done in many countries of the world by the peasants or the *common people*. Traditionally, common folk could not afford to buy or commission works of professional artists, so they painted their walls, tinware and furniture themselves. Thus the term "folk art painting" was coined to describe the more primitive, self-taught style of their work.

Folk art painting is usually done with round brushes, and almost all countries have some type of folk art they can claim as their own. From Norway and its districts come the elegant Telemark, Hallingdal, and Rogaland. From Germany comes Bauernmalerei, from the Netherlands we see Assendelfter and Hindeloopen, from the villages of Russia come Zhostovo florals, and there are many others. The study of the many folk arts of the world is an amazing and never-ending adventure.

Highlights—Highlights are the lightest areas on a painting, implying reflected light.

Linseed Oil—The vehicle into which pigments are mixed to create oil paint. Linseed oil is also used as a painting medium.

Masterson Sta-Wet Palette—A palette containing a sponge and special paper which are soaked in water before acrylics are squeezed onto the palette. This system keeps acrylics wet and workable much longer than a regular palette.

Oil Paint—Oils are pigments ground in linseed oil. They dry slowly, allowing plenty of time for blending and reworking. Oils must be thinned and cleaned up with mineral spirits or turpentine.

Outlining—Painting a thin line around an area or design, done with the point of a round or liner brush.

Overblending—This is a mistake that causes the colors you have applied to turn into a brown, muddy mess.

Paint Consistency—Refers to the thinness or thickness of the paint. Different techniques will require different consistencies.

Pat Blending—Blending with a large flat brush and a light touch to gently merge colors into one another.

Shading—Shading is the use of light and dark colors to create the effect of depth and dimension.

Shadows—Shadows are the dark areas applied where one leaf goes under another leaf or one flower or fruit goes under another one.

Smoking—A decorative finish created by trailing the smoke from a candle across the surface of your project, creating a cloudy black effect.

Sponging—A decorative finish created by dabbing a sponge lightly covered with paint over a basecoated project, creating a dappled texture.

Staining—A thin layer of color is applied to raw wood, enhancing the pattern of the grain, prior to any decorative painting.

Tole Painting—The word *tole* is French for tin or metal; therefore, tole painting only refers to the painting or decoration of tin or metal. Many people say tole painting when they actually should be saying decorative painting.

Turpentine, turps or turpenoid—The solvent for oil paints.

Undercoating—To paint something that is light in color over a dark background, you must first undercoat the area with white paint so that the light color will appear bright and vibrant.

Varnish—Available in a high-gloss or satin finish, and as a water-base or oil-base product. I use both finishes. An oil-base varnish will generally yellow slightly and acrylic varnish will not. Always ask a knowledgeable paint dealer about the type of varnish you should use.

1
Supplies

*S*upplies for decorative painting are readily available all over the world. Maybe not all of the supplies that I'm going to mention in this book, but certainly enough to make it possible for anyone to paint almost anywhere.

If you are new to painting, your first question may be, "Should I paint in acrylics or oils?" Why not both! When I'm teaching people how to paint, that's exactly what I'm doing: I'm teaching them how to paint. Therefore, with just a little fine tuning and understanding of the medium you wish to use, you can paint in oils, acrylics, egg tempera, casein, or watercolor. Really any medium you wish.

Oil Supplies

OIL PAINT

Oil paints are pigments ground in linseed or a similar oil. Oils dry slowly and can be blended beautifully. Some of the pigments, such as the Cadmium colors, are more expensive and magnificently opaque, while some pigments are transparent. It is seldom necessary to undercoat when using oils, because of their opacity.

Oil paints are my favorite painting medium. Regardless of what you've heard, they're very easy to use and very forgiving. They give you the time you need to practice and to memorize a technique. When a technique is learned, practiced and committed to memory, then the technique can be easily performed in acrylics if desired.

SOLVENT

The solvents for oils are turpentine, mineral spirits, odorless turp or one of the new, completely safe solvents on the market, such as Safe Solve, manufactured by the American Color Company, or Turpenoid Natural, manufactured by Martin/F. Weber. At this time, I am still experimenting with the new safe solvents, trying to determine if their performance is satisfactory for my own needs. Some people feel that the low odor turps are not desirable because they are still poisonous. By taking proper precautions and using plain old commonsense, thus far in my thirty years of experience, I have not had any problems using these solvents.

LINSEED OIL

Linseed oil is often the vehicle into which pigments are mixed to create oil paints. Sometimes to give a creamier consistency to my paint I will add a little linseed oil.

JAPAN DRIER

If desired, a small amount of this drier may be added to the oil colors to accelerate drying time.

Tip

When I'm painting with oils, I clean my hands with baby oil rather than turp. I also keep turp covered when I am not cleaning brushes or mixing it into my oil colors; therefore, my exposure to the turp is extremely minimal.

PRISCILLA HAUSER BRUSH CREAM

An excellent cleaner and conditioner for red sable brushes (use for oils only).

BABY OIL

For cleaning your hands when painting with oils.

OTHER SUPPLIES

- A needle-nose bottle for turp
- Tracing paper
- A disposable palette pad

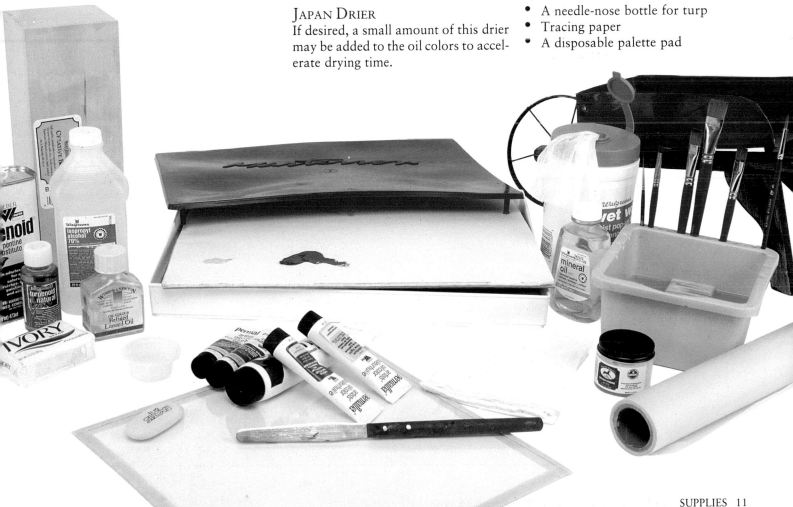

Acrylic Supplies

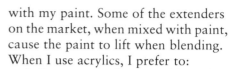

ACRYLIC PAINT

Acrylics are our newest form of paint. They are a polymer emulsion or, in other words, a liquid plastic. Acrylics are water-soluble when they are wet, and they dry quickly. Acrylics are available in both tubes and bottles, in an overwhelming spectrum of colors. I recommend beginners purchase only the pure artist's colors such as Burnt Umber, Burnt Sienna, Cadmium Red Light, Cadmium Red Medium, Cadmium Yellow Light, Cadmium Yellow Medium, Prussian Blue, Titanium White, etc. I recommend a high-quality, thick paint that contains a lot of pigment.

I do not recommend attempting the blending techniques taught in this book with pre-mixed bottled colors. These have been mixed and grayed down to produce subtle color variations. These colors can be very attractive when used as a base coat, trim or for a primitive painting technique—but when you try to blend three or four of these colors, the many colors that make up each pre-mixed color will combine to form an undesirable muddy brown.

Fine art acrylics are a wonderful medium once you know how to paint, but they can be a bit frustrating to a beginner, simply because they dry so fast, and are more transparent than oils. Now, I'm not saying don't begin with acrylics, I just want you to know and understand the assets and liabilities of this medium.

In order for acrylics to stay wet and blendable, you must keep them in a cold, damp surrounding, with no air blowing on them. I always put ice in my water and often a cookie sheet of crushed ice under my wet palette. I keep my studio 68° or colder and never have a fan blowing. If the humidity is high, that's even better. A cold, damp basement with excellent lighting is a pretty good environment for making the acrylics stay wet and blendable.

If your studio is hot and dry with lots of air blowing, then the acrylics will dry too quickly. I rarely use a hair dryer to hasten the drying of the acrylics when basecoating. Wood holds heat, and if I'm going to blend, then I have to wait for the wood to cool down.

ACRYLIC EXTENDERS OR RETARDERS

These are chemicals that are sometimes added to or used with acrylics to help keep them wet. They are commercially marketed under many different names, so always read the small print to see what you are buying. Many companies make what is called a blending medium. This medium is often created by mixing extender, which is thin, with matte medium, which is thick.

Very rarely do I ever mix extender with my paint. Some of the extenders on the market, when mixed with paint, cause the paint to lift when blending. When I use acrylics, I prefer to:

1. Basecoat my design and let it dry. Since acrylics are more transparent than oils, the general rule is to basecoat smoothly and neatly, applying a second coat to cover the surface if needed.

2. Apply a little extender or a painting and blending medium to the area I'm going to paint.

3. Apply paint and blend. If I'm not satisfied with the way my painting looks, I let the paint dry and cure before reworking. Depending upon the drying conditions and the environment you are working in, and the brand of extender you are using, this may take anywhere from thirty minutes to twenty-four hours or more.

MASTERSON STA-WET PALETTE

This piece of equipment is so important to me that if I did not have this palette, I would not want to paint with acrylics. The palette comes in three different sizes; of these I prefer using the largest one, for it gives me more room. Each palette comes with a sponge, which should be thoroughly wet with water, and a special paper that should be soaked at least twenty-four hours before using.

Place the thoroughly soaked paper on top of the very wet sponge. Wipe the paper off with a soft, absorbent paper towel, then place the acrylic colors onto the paper on the palette. When I have finished painting, I wipe the paper off, rinse it and reuse it two and sometimes three times before throwing it away. Of course, the paper will not work if you let the acrylics dry on it.

ACRYLIC BRUSH CLEANER

There are quite a few brush cleaners on the market. Liquid dish soap also works well.

General Supplies

The following items are used for both oil and acrylic painting, in addition to those already mentioned.

- Brush basin
- Tracing paper
- A 12" × 12" (30.5cm × 30.5cm) pane of glass (tape the edges for your protection) or a tile for mixing colors
- A good straight-blade, flexible steel palette knife
- Soft, absorbent cotton rags or towels
- Tack rag
- Wet wipes
- White and colored chalk for pattern transfer
- Alcohol for cleaning the mixing surface

SURFACE PREPARATION AND DECORATIVE FINISHING SUPPLIES

Stain

Staining applies a thin layer of color into the raw wood. Stains are available in water-base or oil-base. I prefer staining with an oil-base stain, because I simply like the finish I get with the oil-base stains, as well as the extra time I have to get the staining done. However, for quick, easy projects, I will occasionally use one of the water-base stains. Carefully read and follow the directions on the container.

Varnish

Varnish is available in a high-gloss finish or a satin finish. It also comes as a water-base or oil-base product. I use both finishes. An oil-base varnish will generally yellow slightly while acrylic varnish usually will not. Always ask a knowledgeable paint dealer about the type of varnish you should use.

Clear Acrylic Spray

Clear acrylic spray is actually a lacquer base with its solvent being acetone. I use it occasionally for sealing a porous surface, but I always use it in a well-ventilated area, for the fumes can be harmful.

Acrylic Basecoat Colors

These are the hundreds of pre-mixed colors found in your local art and craft stores. Remember, do not use these for blending!

Scotch Brand Magic Tape

Use this for banding or trimming the edges of projects.

Crackle Medium

There are two types of crackle medium sold commercially. One is applied over a dry basecoat color. When a contrasting overcoat color is painted on top of the medium, the paint can't adhere properly and therefore breaks up into a crackled pattern, revealing the basecoat beneath. The other is a two-part product which is applied over the finished painting. When the product is dry, it is antiqued, thus revealing the cracks.

Antiquing Glaze

This product is available as a water-base glaze or an oil-base glaze. It is applied over a sealed surface so that you can control the amount you leave on or wipe off. Soft or textured rags are used to wipe the prepared surface, leaving as much or as little of the glaze as desired. This will give an aged look to the piece you are painting.

Additional Supplies

- Sponge brushes
- Sandpaper
- Pieces of unprinted brown paper bag for smoothing surfaces
- Wood sealer
- Other special-effect mediums

Tip

Acrylics do allow the use of water during the blending process. When blending with acrylics, if you feel that they are drying, you can touch the brush to water, blot it on a rag and slightly reactivate the acrylic in order to keep it moving. This technique takes skill that can only be developed with a lot of practice.

Brushes

Your brush is your most important tool. And your painting will be only as good as your brush, so please, buy the best brushes available.

A beginning painter will need both round and flat brushes. For the beginner, I recommend purchasing a no. 2, no. 4, no. 8, no. 10, no. 12 and no. 14 flat brush; a no. 3 round brush; and a no. 1 liner brush. If you are using acrylic paint, I recommend synthetic brushes. If you are painting in oils, I prefer red sable or Kolinsky sable.

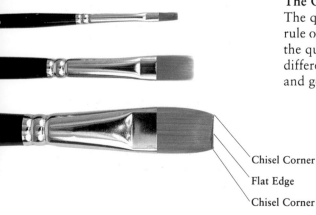

Chisel Corner
Flat Edge
Chisel Corner

ROUND BRUSHES
You'll find many different-shaped brushes in the round brush family. The one thing they all have in common is that the metal ferrule that encases the hair is round. This family includes round watercolor brushes, round oil brushes, filberts, liners and quills. Brushstrokes created with a round brush are very graceful. Round brushes are generally used for stroking and not blending.

Filberts
The filbert brush looks rather like a round brush flattened out and curved on either side. Many people use filberts for brushstrokes.

Liner Brushes
Beautiful comma strokes and polliwogs can be made with the liner brush. Of course, as its name implies, it is primarily used for fine line and detail work.

When painting with the liner brush, be sure that your brush is in excellent condition, and completely full of paint which is of a very thin and flowing consistency. Twist the brush carefully to a point and paint with the brush so that the handle points straight towards the ceiling.

The Quill
The quill is so called because the ferrule of the brush is actually made from the quill of a feather. The quill is a bit different in shape than the liner brush and generally holds more paint. I love to do border work and fine linework with a quill.

FLAT BRUSHES
Flat brushes are used for stroke work as well as blending colors together. The head of a flat brush is generally squared, creating a flat edge (also known as the chisel edge). (When you are painting on the flat edge of the brush, the handle of the brush will point straight up towards the ceiling.) Many different effects can be achieved with a flat brush, from thick stripes or bands of color made by pulling with the flat surface of the brush, to thin lines made with the flat edge. The two sides of the brush are also chisel edges. The corners, I will refer to as chisel corners.

 Tip

If you are farsighted, reading glasses are not painting glasses! The next time you go for glasses, be sure you let your eye doctor know what you are doing. I've had students who couldn't do linework simply because they couldn't see. When I am painting small, delicate things, I wear what is called an Optivisor or surgical loop, which are commonly used by jewelers. These are available where you buy your glasses. I find the Optivisor helpful, although it took a while to get used to wearing it. If you suspect you need more magnification, ask your eye doctor about one.

SPECIAL-EFFECT BRUSHES

You will find many special-effect brushes in the stores. Some of them are useful and some of them, in my opinion, are not so useful. There are fan brushes, rakes and others. In my own painting, I don't find the addition of many of these brushes particularly helpful. However, on occasion, when painting fur or hair, I will use a rake brush. If you see an unusual brush and would love to give it a try, then for goodness sake, buy it, give it a try and, if you like it, add it to your collection.

BRUSH CARE AND CLEANING

Because of your large investment in the purchase of fine-quality brushes, as well as the need for their excellent performance, it is extremely important to care for them properly. Before you begin to paint with a new brush, you must "break it in." Most brushes come with sizing in them to help the brush keep its shape. It is necessary to wash out all of the sizing and to rinse the brush in water before you use it.

Synthetic Brushes

When you are finished painting, rinse the brush in water as thoroughly as possible. Squeeze a little liquid detergent or brush cleaner into a small container and work the brush back and forth until all of the paint is removed. Then shape your brush, leaving the cleaner in the hairs, and store it with the hairs up. The next time you are ready to paint, simply rinse the brush to remove the cleaner.

Sable Brushes

Always clean your brushes after you have finished painting for the day. If proper care is taken, brushes will last quite a long time. To clean a brush, stroke it gently back and forth in your turp. Never abuse or break the hairs of the brush.

After washing the brush well in turp, place a dab of Priscilla Hauser Brush Cream in the lid of the jar. As you work the brush back and forth in the brush cream, you will see the paint come out of the hairs. Wipe the brush on a soft rag and rinse the brush again in turp, then stroke gently back and forth on a bar of Ivory Soap. Work up a good lather.

Leave the soap in the brush and shape it with your fingers until every hair is in place. The soap serves as sizing and helps keep the brush in good condition. Soap will not harm the brush, the turp or the paint. Before using the brush again, gently rinse it in turp.

Tip

A beginning student and sometimes even an advanced painter can abuse brushes.

- Don't ever grind the brush in your brush basin when cleaning it. Be sure the basin contains plenty of turp or water.
- The rag you wipe your brush on is very important. It should be very soft and absorbent. Rub your knuckles firmly on the rag—does it hurt? If not, your rag is probably soft enough to wipe your brushes on. People don't realize what they do to a brush if they are using a coarse, rough rag or toweling. Soft, 100% cotton rags or very absorbent paper toweling is always the best.
- Remember, when storing sable or natural hair brushes, you will want to toss in some moth balls. Roaches, silverfish and rodents love to eat the hairs of your brushes.

2
Surface Preparations and Finishes

Properly preparing and finishing your project's surface will ensure that the beautiful decorative work you add to it will last for many years. This chapter also includes a variety of decorative finishing techniques—such as antiquing and striping—that will pull your project together and give it a charming, polished appeal.

Staining Wood

Staining means to apply a thin glaze of paint to a raw wood surface. Since the stain is transparent, it does not cover the grain of the wood as painting does, but rather accentuates the wood's natural patterns. Commercial stains often offer a selection of natural tones that make less expensive wood such as pine resemble one of the richer grains like cherry or oak. In addition to these traditional brown hues, wood can be stained a rainbow of different colors from white (called pickling), to pastel or any combination of colors desired.

If I were going to stain large, unfinished pieces, I would probably go to a name brand paint store and purchase a very high-quality wood stain in the color of my choice, so that all the pieces would match. However, for smaller items, I always create my own stain, simply because I like what I make better than what I can buy in a store. The choice is yours.

OILS

1. Sand the piece, if needed.

2. Wipe with a tack rag.

3. Using a rag or sponge brush, wipe the piece of wood to be stained with just a little turp. This will allow the oil color to flow on smoothly.

4. Mix a little oil color and turp together on a palette or in a small bowl. The proportions aren't particularly important. If you want a darker stain, use more paint and less turp; a lighter stain requires more turp, less paint. Brush the stain onto the wood.

5. Wipe the stain off using soft rags or towels.

6. You may wish to darken the edges of the wood; this really enhances the finished effect. To do this, apply a small amount of Burnt Umber all the way around the outside edge of the board. Use a circular motion and rub the Burnt Umber into the wood using the flat part of your finger.

7. Blend the darkened edge into the rest of the stain by folding a soft rag and rubbing around the edge of the dark stain, creating a gradual blending from the dark to medium to light.

ACRYLICS

The process for staining wood with acrylics is essentially the same as above, except you don't apply linseed oil to the surface first. Use a sponge brush to apply a generous amount of stain to the wood and brush quickly, using long even strokes. If you wish the stain to be darker or more intense, apply a second coat.

Painting Wood

Another option for preparing wood for decorative painting is to paint it with oils or acrylics. I like to use the acrylic basecoat colors (pre-mixed, bottled acrylics) because they dry fast and clean up with water. There are wonderful colors available in arts and crafts, hardware and fabric stores. I use sponge brushes for applying acrylic paint. They're easy to clean up, inex-pensive and can be thrown away once you have finished using them.

A third option is to paint directly on the raw wood. To prepare the wood for this technique, simply sand the wood and wipe with a tack rag as shown in steps one and two below, then transfer your design to the surface.

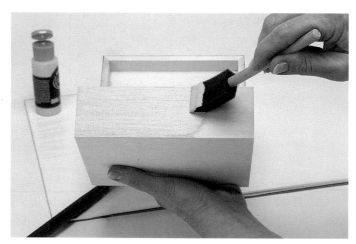

1. Sand the wood, if necessary, until smooth.

2. Wipe with a tack rag.

3. Using a sponge brush, apply a generous amount of paint. Work quickly and use a light touch.

4. Let the paint dry. Rub with a piece of brown paper bag that has no printing on it to smooth the wood grain. I often use this method rather than sand paper, as it beautifully smoothes the surface and is nonabrasive. Apply a second coat of acrylic base-coat, if needed. Sometimes, more than one or two coats are needed depending upon the transparency or opacity of the paint.

Sealing Wood

To seal or not to seal? There are many different theories on if and when you should seal. My rule is this. If I'm going to basecoat a piece of wood that has knotholes in it, or wood that I suspect is green, I will seal it before basecoating or staining to keep discoloration from bleeding through. But if the wood is properly aged and cured, then I prefer not to seal before staining or basecoating because the paint bonds to unsealed wood much better.

What about after the wood is basecoated or stained, but prior to decorative painting? If you're doing your decorative painting in oils, seal the surface. The oils will soak into the basecoated or unsealed stained wood and you won't be able to properly move them.

If you're painting with acrylics, the choice is yours. I used to always seal lightly before doing my decorative painting with acrylics because if I made a mistake or dropped a brush it was a little bit easier to remove the paint. But I don't do that anymore. I simply transfer my pattern to the painted surface and then do my decorative painting in acrylics.

I can keep the acrylic paint wetter a little longer by applying a painting or blending medium to the unsealed surface. If the surface has been sealed, the painting and blending medium dries very quickly, thus requiring you to blend much faster.

For sealing, my favorite product is a properly thinned clear shellac. If I want to spray seal, I use many light coats of a clear acrylic spray. There are so many sealers on the market today that it can be a difficult decision for the decorative painter. Product information and excellent instructions are essential.

As a general rule, I only seal wood prior to basecoating or staining if it is green or has knotholes that might show through the paint. Seal wood after basecoating or staining but prior to decorative painting if you're using oils to paint your decorative design.

Clear acrylic spray can be used to seal a finished piece, but only in a well-ventilated area.

Preparing Tin

Before tole painting, you need to prepare your tin and metal pieces so that paint will adhere properly to them.

1. The first thing I do for old tin pieces is make a thin paste of dishwasher detergent and water. Cover the item with this paste and let it set for about thirty minutes. (Please wear rubber gloves when applying the paste as dishwasher detergent can take the skin right off your hands.)

2. When the detergent has had time to work, scrub the metal with a steel wool pad, rinse with water and dry thoroughly.

3. To remove any rust from old pieces, purchase a good rust remover from a quality paint store and follow the manufacturer's instructions.

4. Prior to painting, the metal must be properly primed. There are good primers on the market, but I prefer to take my tinware to an automobile body shop. These people are experts at making paint adhere to metal, and often when they are getting ready to put a primer on a car they will spray my metal pieces as well. Always be sure to find out what type of paint—lacquer base, oil base or acrylic base—can be used on top of the primer if your primer color is not going to be used as the basecoat.

5. Basecoat over the primer, if desired. Let dry, and add your decorative designs.

Preparing Fabric

Preparation of fabric for decorative painting is relatively easy.

1. First wash the fabric, if possible, to remove any sizing from it. If the item you are going to paint will never be washed after you add your design, this step isn't necessary.

2. Neatly transfer your design. My favorite method for transferring a pattern onto fabric is to use chalk—white for dark fabrics and colored chalk for light fabrics. Charcoal pencils will also work well. Neatly trace the pattern onto tracing paper, turn it over and firmly go over the back of the lines with chalk. Shake off the excess chalk dust. Center the pattern on the fabric and hold it in place. Then scrape a plastic credit card across the pattern using a great deal of pressure. This will press the chalked pattern onto the fabric.

3. If you are using a loose piece of fabric, firmly attach it to a piece of foamcore board that has been cut to the appropriate size. To prevent spills and stray marks from spoiling the rest of the fabric, place the whole project in a plastic bag. Now cut out a window over the area to which the decorative painting will be applied and tape the edges of the plastic down.

4. You are now ready to add your decorative painting. I rarely use fabric mediums (paints, markers, etc.) when I paint on fabric. I simply mix my oils or acrylics to the proper consistency.

5. **For Acrylics**—Apply a little painting and blending medium to the fabric. Be careful not to get too close to the edges of the design in order to avoid paint bleeding outside the design area. As long as the fabric stays wet with medium, the acrylics will stay wet and allow you to paint and blend beautifully.

6. **For Oils**—Apply a little gel medium to the fabric. This medium is available wherever oil paints are sold. The gel medium fills any texture in the fabric, allowing the oil paint to flow onto the fabric beautifully.

7. When dry, I heat set the oils. This is not necessary with acrylics. Dampen the dried fabric with white vinegar. This helps set any colors that might not be permanent. Lay a pressing cloth over the oils and iron the painted area. Hang to dry.

Tip

I believe hand-painted items should be hand-washed. Save machine washing for machine-made fabrics. If I have spent the time to do a beautiful job painting something, I don't want to destroy it by using a washer or dryer. However, the choice is yours.

Trace the pattern on to tracing paper, then go over the back of the design with chalk.

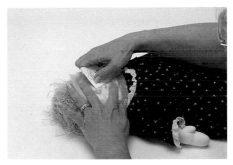

Hold the pattern in place, chalk side down, and scrape over it with a credit card.

The chalk pattern is transferred to the fabric.

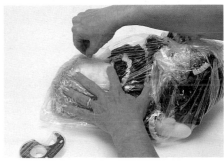

Put the entire piece into a plastic bag to protect it, cut a window over the area you will be painting, and tape the edges down.

Preparing Paper

Although paper doesn't require much preparation, it generally has to be sealed pretty well before decorative painting can be applied on it. I usually seal the paper using many light coats of clear acrylic spray. Occasionally, I will transfer my design to the paper and, using a small brush, seal only the design area before doing the decorative painting.

Preparing Glass

Glass can be painted with oils or acrylics; using acrylics is simply a matter of proper preparation.

1. Wash the glass carefully and dry it thoroughly.

2. If it isn't clear glass, you can mist it lightly with a little clear acrylic spray to give it some "tooth" for the paint to adhere to. Clear glass cannot be treated in this way because the acrylic spray will show.

3. Transfer your design.

4. If you are using oils, you are now ready to paint. Use a very thick consistency of paint and a light touch when blending.

5. If you are using acrylics, you will need to etch the pattern onto the glass with an etching creme, such as Barb's Glass Etching Solution. This will give tooth to the glass and make painting it much easier. Another option is to first paint the design area using Jo Sonya's All Purpose Sealer, then apply your acrylics.

6. When finished, I usually varnish only the painted design rather than the whole piece. If you have chosen to paint an opaque or colored glass, you may choose to varnish the entire piece.

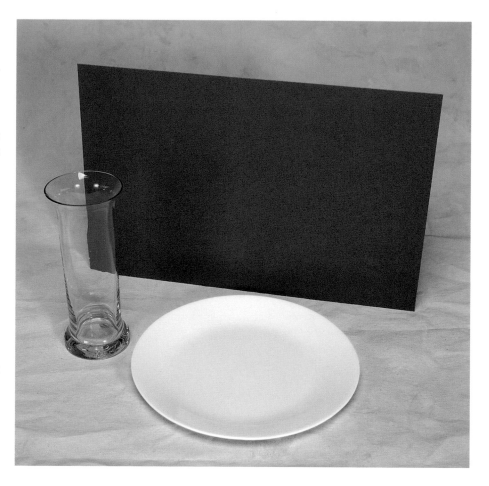

Preparing Plastic

1. Wash the plastic with dish soap, and then neatly and carefully transfer the design.

2. If your piece has a glossy finish, it might be helpful to lightly sand the area where the design will be painted. This will give the surface "tooth" for the paint to adhere to.

3. I recommend testing a small area of the plastic first to be sure your oils or acrylic products do not soften or melt the plastic. Some types of plastic will soften while others will not.

Decorative Finishes and Trims

Accenting your projects with decorative finishes and colorful trims is like icing on the cake. Choosing the proper trims and finishes, while they take time, will make or break your decorative painting.

Materials for acrylic antiquing.

Materials for oil antiquing.

Antiquing

Antiquing is a technique that can be used for aging a piece. It is a process of wiping a glaze of thinned brown or black paint over your finished piece to create a soft, aged look. Subtle antiquing can also warm up stark projects and tone down over-bright colors.

Pre-mixed glazes are available in water and oil bases. To create your own oil-base glaze, simply use three parts turp to one part linseed oil, to which you add the desired oil color or colors. The steps for application are the same for both mediums, except that oil-base glazes allow you more time for applying and wiping off than acrylics.

1. Basecoat the piece to be antiqued in the desired color or colors. It's a good idea to apply the glaze over a sealed surface so you can control the amount you leave on or wipe off.

2. Apply the glaze with a sponge brush.

3. Using a soft, lint-free cotton cloth, wipe the glaze back off, leaving darker areas around edges and in niches. Texture can be achieved by varying the fabrics you wipe with. Try cheesecloth, old nylon hose, corduroy, etc. Wipe most of the glaze off for a subtle antiqued finish, or leave the glaze darker for a heavily aged look. You can also rub off all the glaze in certain areas to create highlights. If you wipe off too much glaze, simply re-apply and rub with the cloth to blend.

4. Varnish the finished project with a compatible sealer and allow to dry.

Wipe the glaze on with a sponge brush.

Here, an oil glaze is being applied.

Rub the glaze off with a soft cloth. You will need to do this more quickly with acrylics than you would if using an oil-base glaze. Notice that the oil glaze at right is richer in color than the acrylic.

Banding and Striping

Often people think it is difficult to make a straight stripe or band. With practice, it can be done with a liner or striping brush. However, you can use Scotch Brand Magic Tape, in the needed width, and make all kinds of stripes very easily.

1. Using a ruler or hem gauge, measure and mark onto the prepared surface the width of the straight line you wish to follow. Do this with a pencil or a piece of chalk.

2. Next, apply tape along the outside of your marks. The width between the two pieces can be as wide as you desire.

3. Be sure to push the edges of the tape down firmly to keep the paint from crawling underneath.

4. Using a small synthetic or sponge brush, paint the exposed area between the tape. Apply a second, and even a third coat, if needed.

5. If you're banding with acrylics, carefully remove the tape while the paint is still wet. If you have used relatively new tape, and put the edges down firmly, you will have a neat, straight line. If not, you will have to go back and touch up a bit. A little alcohol will sometimes help remove acrylic paint, if it hasn't dried too much.

Measure and draw the line with a straightedge.

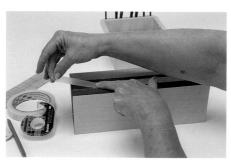

Apply tape along the outside of the line.

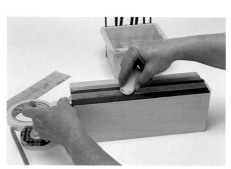

Press the edges of the tape down firmly with a rubber eraser.

Paint the area you wish to band.

Remove the tape before the paint is completely dry.

If you're not sure what color or colors you want to band or stripe in, tape a few strips of Scotch Brand Magic Tape to a piece of plastic and paint them in several different colors. Then tape them in place on your piece to see if you have a color that works properly for your project. You can also use different colors and widths of ribbon to check trim colors and sizes.

Crackling

There are several brands of crackle medium available. They are easy to use, but the directions must be carefully followed.

1. Basecoat with the acrylic color of your choice. Remember that this color will show through the cracks that will form in the top coat. Let dry.

2. Apply the crackle medium rather heavily. Wait the appropriate amount of time as given in the directions for the crackle medium you use.

3. Apply the contrasting acrylic topcoat color. Only brush over each area of the surface once.

Apply crackle glaze to the basecoated project.

Cracks will begin to appear as you apply a top coat over the crackle medium.

Flyspecking

You can flyspeck with one, or as many colors as you desire. There are many ways to flyspeck, and you should use whatever technique works best for you. I prefer using an old toothbrush. The consistency of the paint is most important—not too thick or too thin. Experiment on a brown grocery bag or piece of paper to get the size flyspecks you desire.

1. Fill an old toothbrush with paint by rubbing the bristles into the desired color.

2. Pull your thumb over the bristles, allowing paint droplets to sprinkle to the surface below. Sometimes I wear a rubber glove when I do this. With practice, you will find you can control the direction in which the flyspecks fall. The specks should vary in size.

Pull your thumb over the bristles to create a fine spatter of paint droplets.

Smoking

Smoking has been used for generations to create a quick and easy marbleized finish. The technique is added to a basecoated surface, and works best on a light background.

1. To achieve the effect, firmly anchor a candle in a safe candle holder. Light the candle and put the end of a steel palette knife into the tip of the flame. Practice this and watch the black smoke begin to curl. The more sooty the tip of the knife becomes, the better the smoke.

2. Carefully hold the basecoated piece above the smoke. The smoke will dance and curl creating a marble-like effect on the painted surface. When finished, seal the smoked surface using several light coats of clear acrylic spray.

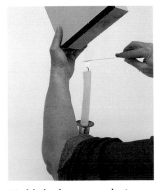

Hold the basecoated piece above the flame, then swirl the smoke with the palette knife.

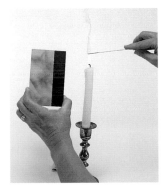

The smoke creates a cloudy marbled finish on your surface.

Sponging

Many wonderful, mottled effects can be achieved by sponging. This technique can be done with a sea sponge or a household sponge.

1. Basecoat the area you wish to sponge with a contrasting color. You can sponge a dark color over a lighter one, or a light color onto a dark background. Here I am sponging black over a deep green for a subtle effect. I've chosen a natural sea sponge for this project, as it creates a more textural effect than a household sponge.

2. Dip the sponge in water and squeeze out the excess.

3. Squeeze the desired colors onto a wax-coated palette or wax-coated paper. Dip the sponge into the paint and blot several times on the palette to remove the excess.

4. Sponge the surface of your piece using an up-and-down motion. After you have made your first sponge mark, lift the sponge off the surface and then turn it slightly before touching it to your project again. This will prevent the holes in the sponge from forming a regular pattern of marks as you work.

5. Cover the entire area you wish to sponge. You may need to use a corner, or cut off a small piece of sponge to work the paint into small areas or along edges that border areas you don't want to be sponged. If you get too much paint in any area, let the paint dry, then go back over that area with your basecoat color.

1. Materials needed for sponging.

2. Wet the sponge and squeeze almost dry.

3. Dip the sponge into the paint and blot several times on the palette to remove the excess paint.

4. Sponge the surface using an up-and-down motion.

5. Don't forget to press, lift, turn and press to prevent a regular pattern of sponge marks from forming.

Finishing a Project

Varnishing does two things: It brings up the color of paint which has dried flat, giving it a lovely finish, and it protects your piece from wear and weathering. Varnishes come in water and oil bases, and in indoor and outdoor formulas. The following finishes should be applied only after all decorative painting and decorative finish techniques have been completed and allowed to dry and cure.

WATER-BASE FINISHES

When I apply a water-base varnish, I often use a sponge brush—they're really wonderful tools. Water-base varnish can be applied over oils or acrylics. That's right, I said over oils. However, the oils must be dried and cured. Cured means the paint must be dried throughout the thickness of the paint. This takes time and no one can tell you exactly how long because it depends on the drying environment.

If the water-base varnish beads up when you apply it over the oils, don't panic. Let the varnish dry, then firmly rub the surface with a piece of brown paper bag that has no printing on it. The second coat of varnish should flow smoothly over the paint.

1. Brush the water-base varnish on rather generously and as quickly as possible. Let it dry.

2. Apply second and third coats, allowing them to dry in between coats. Let the third coat dry completely.

3. Sand lightly with fine wet-and-dry trimite paper, or rub with a piece of brown paper bag that has no printing on it.

4. Apply a final coat of varnish.

OIL-BASE FINISHES

Most oil-base varnishes contain linseed oil. Therefore, they will yellow or mellow over time. Often this patina adds an attractive aged quality to the piece, but it may not be desirable if the background is white or a pastel color. This should be taken into consideration when choosing which type of finish to use.

I apply oil-base varnish in the same way as water-base. Always be sure each coat has dried thoroughly before applying another coat.

OUTDOOR FINISHES

I'm often asked which is the best product to use on something that will be displayed outside. The answer is "Nothing is permanent." Any decorative accessory used outdoors should be brought in once a year, thoroughly cleaned, lightly sanded and revarnished. Often I use a paste wax, such as Johnson's Floor Wax, applied over the varnish to help weatherproof an outdoor piece. Here are some helpful suggestions.

1. Polyurethane yellows; if this doesn't matter, a good marine finish works well. Be sure your paint is thoroughly dried and cured before applying such a finish, or you could cause a chemical reaction to occur, which could make your paint crack.

2. Water-base finishes generally do not yellow, and therefore are preferable for pieces that have a light-colored background that you do not want to yellow with age. While not as durable as marine finishes, with proper care and yearly refreshing, they will serve you well.

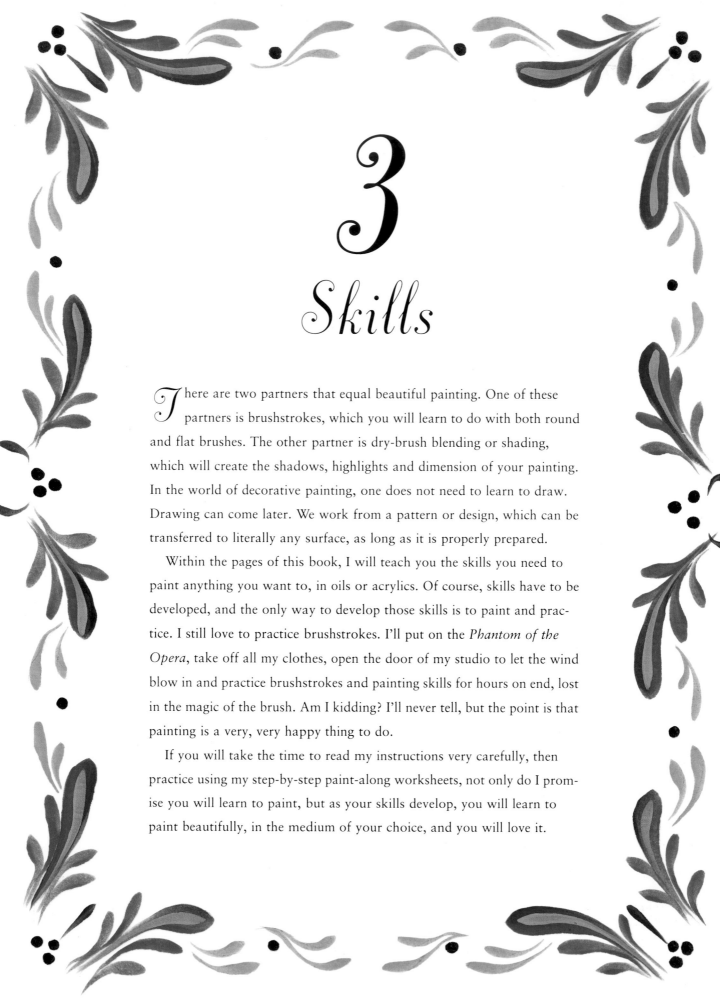

3
Skills

There are two partners that equal beautiful painting. One of these partners is brushstrokes, which you will learn to do with both round and flat brushes. The other partner is dry-brush blending or shading, which will create the shadows, highlights and dimension of your painting. In the world of decorative painting, one does not need to learn to draw. Drawing can come later. We work from a pattern or design, which can be transferred to literally any surface, as long as it is properly prepared.

Within the pages of this book, I will teach you the skills you need to paint anything you want to, in oils or acrylics. Of course, skills have to be developed, and the only way to develop those skills is to paint and practice. I still love to practice brushstrokes. I'll put on the *Phantom of the Opera*, take off all my clothes, open the door of my studio to let the wind blow in and practice brushstrokes and painting skills for hours on end, lost in the magic of the brush. Am I kidding? I'll never tell, but the point is that painting is a very, very happy thing to do.

If you will take the time to read my instructions very carefully, then practice using my step-by-step paint-along worksheets, not only do I promise you will learn to paint, but as your skills develop, you will learn to paint beautifully, in the medium of your choice, and you will love it.

Basecoating

There are two types of basecoating. One is to paint an entire piece of wood, tin or other surface with two or three coats of paint that will serve as the base color of the project, prior to adding any decorative painting.

Basecoating also refers to the filling in or undercoating of the actual transferred design area, such as the petals of a flower. Basecoats should always be applied as smoothly and evenly as possible.

Basecoating the project.

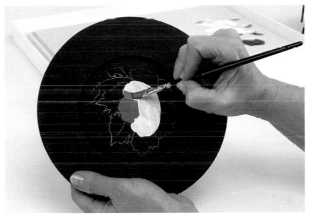

Basecoating the design area.

Transferring a Pattern

There are many ways to do this, and correctly transferring the pattern is an important step. I do not like to use graphite carbon to transfer my patterns as it is almost impossible to remove. I prefer to use a chalk method.

1. Using tracing paper and a pencil, carefully trace your pattern.

2. Once you have traced your pattern, turn it over and carefully trace over the back of the pattern with white chalk or a chalk pencil. Shake off any excess chalk dust.

3. Place the pattern on the surface to be painted, chalk side down. You may secure it with tape, if necessary. Then, using a pencil or a stylus, neatly retrace the lines of the design. Do not press too hard when retracing or you will make an indentation in the wood. If the background color is light, substitute either brown or green chalk for the white.

Trace the pattern.

Trace over the back with chalk.

Chalk-side down, trace over design again to transfer the chalk to your surface.

Undercoating for Coverage

To paint something that is light in color on a dark background, you may want to undercoat before painting the subject. I seldom undercoat when using oils because they are much more opaque than acrylics.

1. For instance, before painting yellow tulips on a black background, undercoat the petals carefully, smoothly and evenly with white paint. You must stay exactly within the pattern lines and the paint must be perfectly smooth or the undercoat will show through the finished painting.

2. Let the paint dry thoroughly. Apply a second coat, if needed, to

Fill in the design area with white, being careful to stay within the pattern lines.

cover and let dry.

3. Then apply a coat of yellow over the white. The tulip will appear light

Now apply the desired color over the basecoat.

and vivid because of the opaque undercoat.

Outlining

Outlining is used to create a thin line around a design area or as a decorative flourish. Using the fine point of a round brush or a liner brush, completely fill the brush with very thin paint. Twist the brush to a point and then outline the object using a light touch, applying as little pressure as possible to the brush. The handle of the brush should point straight up!

Use very thin paint to create flowing lines.

Consistency

Consistency refers to the thinness or thickness of the paint. It describes the way the paint feels when you mix it with turpentine, low-odor turp, or linseed oil if using oils; or water, if using acrylics. We will use three main consistencies for all the techniques taught in this book.

Heavy Cream or Thick
Generally the paint will squeeze from the tubes of a high-quality oil or acrylic paint in this consistency. I do not recommend using acrylics that are too thin or runny. If you are using tube paints, it may be necessary to add enough water or turp to the paint until it moves easily when you spread it with your palette knife. If you're using bottle acrylics, the paint is thinner and will require no water. This is the consis-

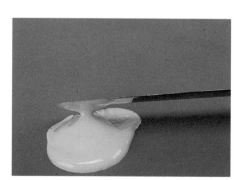

Thick consistency

tency we often use for blending. If the paint is too thin, it is easy to overblend and make mud.

Bird Blessings or Thin, Creamy
This consistency requires mixing the vehicle—water or turp—into your paint until it "plops" off the palette knife like bird blessings. When we are painting brushstrokes, the paint must be a very thin flowing consistency, so the paint will fill the hairs of the brush and then flow smoothly and evenly to the surface we are painting.

Thin, creamy consistency

Inklike consistency

Ink Consistency
For outlining and fine linework it is necessary to have the paint flow from the hairs of a fine liner brush just as ink would flow from a fountain pen. This consistency is also used for curlicues, striping and dots.

Brushstrokes

Oh, please, please learn to paint brushstrokes! They are the alphabet of decorative painting. Brushstrokes may be created with round, flat and filbert brushes. They may be painted in oils, acrylics, watercolors, or whatever medium you desire. Three things are required to learn how to paint beautiful brushstrokes:

- A good brush that is in excellent condition. It is easiest for most people to practice brushstrokes with a medium-sized brush.
- Proper paint consistency.
- A commitment to sit down and practice.

In this section you will learn some of the fundamental strokes. There are many, many variations of these brushstrokes and as our skills develop, we will use these strokes and their variations in the creation of things we paint.

Once you have read through the different strokes, use the worksheet at the end of this section to help you learn to paint brushstrokes. Lay a sheet of acetate over the worksheet and practice your brushstrokes right on top of mine, literally hundreds of times. That's right! I said hundreds, and it won't hurt you a bit, for that's what it takes to really execute these magnificent strokes.

PALETTE PREPARATION

If you are painting with acrylics, I suggest using the Masterson Sta-Wet Palette. If using oils, I use a disposable tracing paper palette pad. To mix the paints to the proper consistency, use a large tile or a 12″ × 12″ (30.5cm × 30.5cm) piece of glass with the edges taped so they won't cut you.

Squeeze a color, such as Leaf Green or Burnt Umber on to the mixing palette; then thin the paint to the proper consistency using a good, straight-blade, steel palette knife. You need to be able to feel the consistency of the paint with the knife. If you are using acrylics, thin the paint with water. If using oils, thin the paint with odorless turp or one of the new safe solvents for oil paint. The paint must be mixed to the consistency of what I have endearingly called "bird blessings." In other words, very loose. When the brush is filled with paint, the paint must flow smoothly and evenly from the hairs of the brush. Most people, in the beginning, try to paint brushstrokes using very thick paint and they are unhappy with the results.

To prime the brush, if using oils, I work a small amount of linseed oil back and forth in the hairs of the brush and then wipe the brush on a rag before filling it with paint. It is not necessary to prime a synthetic brush.

With your palette knife, move the paint you have mixed on your glass or tile to the palette pad. Then fill your brush by stroking it back and forth in the paint. You do not want the brush to run out of paint when you are creating a brushstroke.

Flat Brush Strokes

Let's identify the parts of a flat brush. (You can refer to the photo on page 14.) I call the straight line formed by the very tips of the hairs the flat edge; the corners I refer to as chisel corners. I recommend placing a tape flag on the handle of your brush. This way you can tell if you are twisting or turning the brush in your fingers. In most cases, you do not want the flag to "wave" while you are painting brush strokes.

BASIC STROKE

The first stroke is a basic stroke, it is the easiest stroke to paint. To create this stroke, touch the flat edge to the acetate or practice surface, apply pressure on the flat surface and pull the brush toward you.

LINE STROKE

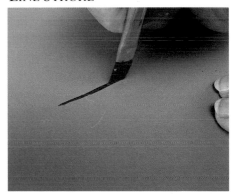

The second stroke is called a line stroke. Stand the brush on the flat edge, with the handle pointing straight up toward the ceiling, and pull the brush toward you, painting a thin line. Don't work on the corner of the brush, but on the flat edge.

Flat Brush Strokes

Comma Stroke

To create a stroke that angles to the left, angle your brush to the left corner of your pratice sheet. Then touch, apply pressure slowly, lift and pull until you lift back onto the flat edge of the brush and drag to form a point. To paint a comma stroke that goes to the right, simply reverse the technique.

Tip

Be sure you turn your practice sheet so that it is in a comfortable position for you to paint. Don't make your arm and hand conform to a practice sheet that's sitting straight on the table. You will notice in the following demonstrations my practice sheet is turned 90° to the right.

Flat Brush Right

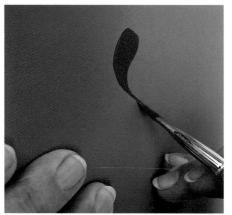

1. To create a stroke that angles to the right, angle your brush to the right corner of your practice sheet. Then touch and apply pressure slowly.

2. Lift and pull toward you, gradually lifting and leaning to the right inside edge of the brush until you lift back onto the flat edge of the brush.

3. Drag the flat edge of the brush to the right to form the comma's tail, lifting the brush cleanly off the paper to form a point.

Flat Brush Left

1. To paint a comma stroke that goes to the left, simply reverse the technique. Angle your brush to the left corner, touch and apply pressure slowly.

2. Lift and pull toward you, gradually angling your stroke to the left until you lift back onto the flat edge of the brush.

3. Drag the flat edge of the brush to the left and lift off to form a point.

S-STROKE

The S-stroke makes an attractive decorative flourish for borders. When angled to the right, it resembles an *S*, but it can also be reversed and angled to the left. I've found it's easier for a right-handed student to paint strokes that angle to the left and for a left-handed student to paint strokes that angle to the right.

Right

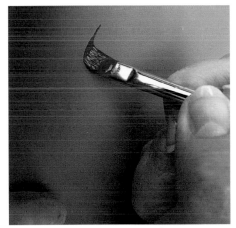 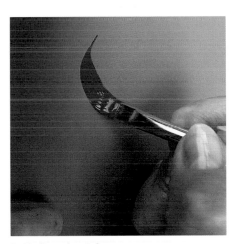 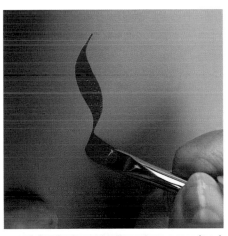

1. To create an S-stroke that angles to the right, stand the brush on the flat edge and slide gently, letting the brush roll to the right.

2. Pull to the right.

3. Lift back up on the flat edge as you finish the stroke.

Left

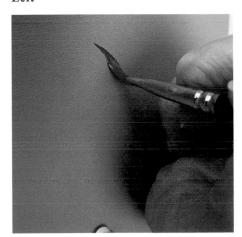 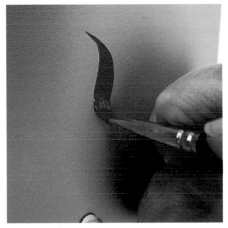 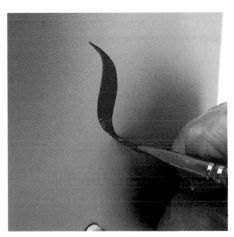

1. Stand the brush on the flat edge and slide gently, letting the brush roll to the left.

2. Pull to the left.

3. Lift back up on the flat edge to finish.

Flat Brush Strokes

U-STROKE
The U-stroke can also be reversed to
create an upside-down *U*. The stroke
is painted with a flat brush.

Rightside Up

1. Stand the brush on the flat edge and slide toward you.

2. Gradually apply pressure until you've reached the bottom of the U, with full pressure on the brush.

3. Gradually begin releasing pressure on the brush as you work back up the other side, until you are back up on the flat edge.

Upside Down

1. Stand the brush on the flat edge and slide away from you.

2. Gradually apply pressure until you've reached the top of the U.

3. Gradually release pressure as you work down the other side.

HALF-CIRCLE STROKE

Half circles can be used on their own or combined to create a nicely formed circle in less time than it takes to fill in a circle with freehand strokes. This is the only stroke in which the flag on the handle of your brush is allowed to wave (see page 38), since the brush will be turning in your fingers. To create this stroke, I usually hold the brush a little higher on the handle, so I can easily pivot the brush in my fingers.

Upside Down

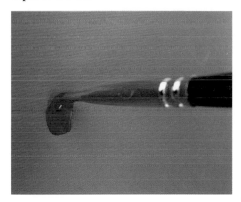

1. Stand the brush on its flat edge. This edge should be horizontal.

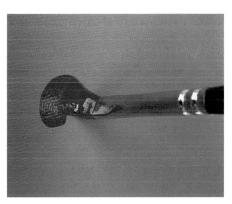

2. Apply pressure and pivot the brush over and to the right.

3. Pivot the flat edge of the brush back to a horizontal position.

Rightside Up

1. Stand the brush with its flat edge horizontal.

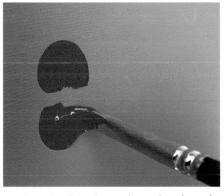

2. Pivot the flat edge under and to the right.

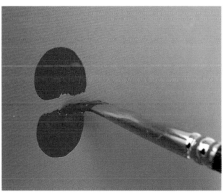

3. Bring the flat edge back to a horizontal position.

Round Brush Strokes

COMMA STROKE

Primarily there are three strokes I will teach you using the round brush, the comma stroke, the polliwog and the curlique, and many variations of these strokes. I prefer using the round watercolor brush with a short handle. The paint consistency remains the same.

After removing any sizing or brush cream, fill the round brush good and full of thin paint.

Round Brush Right

To paint a comma stroke angled to the right, angle the head of the brush toward the right corner of your worksheet.

Apply pressure, begin to pull toward you.

Gradually lift the brush, leaning to the inside edge of the brush until you've reached a point.

Round Brush Left

To paint a comma stroke angled to the left, reverse the technique. Angle the head of the brush toward the left corner.

Apply pressure, begin to pull toward you.

Gradually lift the brush, leaning to the inside edge of the brush until you've reached a point.

Liner Brush

To paint a comma stroke angled to the left with the liner brush, follow the same procedure as with the round brush.

Apply pressure, begin to pull toward you.

Gradually lift the brush leaning to the inside edge of the brush until you've reached a point.

To paint a comma stroke angled to the right, reverse the technique.

POLLIWOG STROKE

The polliwog is very similar to the comma stroke, except that the head is larger and the tail is pulled straight down, rather than angling to the left or right.

Round Brush

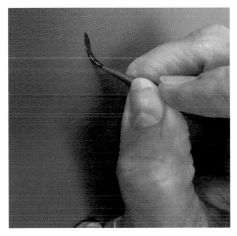 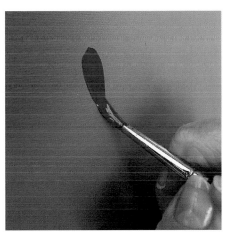 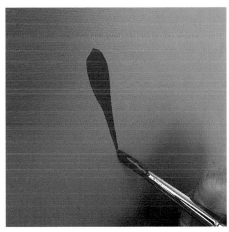

1. Touch the brush to the surface and wiggle it, forcing the hairs to spread out, then gradually pull the brush toward you.

2. Lift as you pull toward you.

3. Form a point by lifting the brush off the surface.

Liner Brush

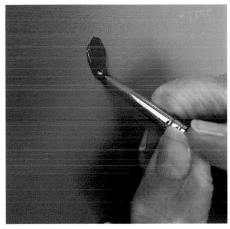 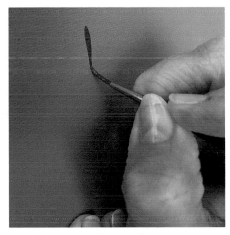 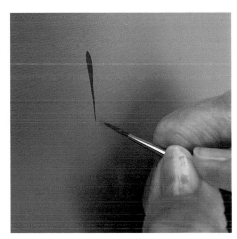

1. Apply pressure to spread the hairs.

2. Lift as you pull toward you.

3. Bring the tail to a point. Notice how much thinner this stroke is when made with the liner brush.

Round Brush Strokes

CURLIQUE

Paint curlicues or squiggles—wonderful for vines and simple ribbons—by filling the liner brush completely full of very thin paint, so the paint will flow from the hairs of the brush just as ink would flow from a fountain pen. Practice making an "M" and then a "W." Put the "Ms" and "Ws" together and you will find that you're doing beautiful curlicues. When painting curlicues or linework, the handle must point straight up toward the ceiling.

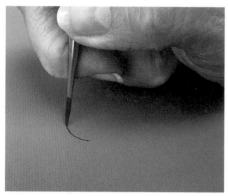

1. *Start with the first hump of a rounded "M."*

2. *Make a loop for the middle leg of the "M."*

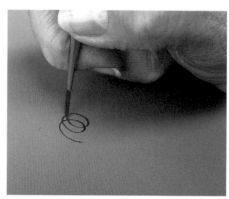

3. *Here I've added a second loop that overlaps my first one.*

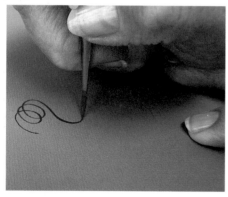

4. *Finish the second hump of the "M," and curve it down to make a bowl as though you were going to paint an exaggerated "W."*

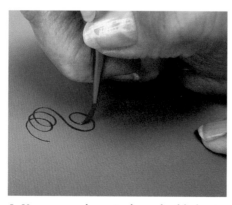

5. *You can make a single or double loop for the center leg of the "W."*

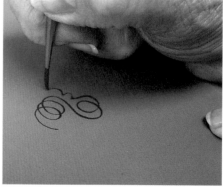

6. *As you finish the second bowl of the "W," wiggle your brush back and forth as you pull upward to create a wavy line. Curliques are freeform. Do your own thing!*

Using the Worksheets

To practice painting brushstrokes and blending, I have provided step-by-step worksheet pages for you to paint over. By painting your strokes right on top of mine, you will understand how each stroke forms the finished effect.

Simply place a clear sheet of acetate on top of the worksheet pages in this book and follow the instructions, matching your strokes to mine. The acetate can then be wiped with solvent and reused.

As you're practicing these techniques, remember to place a tape flag on the handle of your brush. This way you can tell if you are twisting or turning the brush in your fingers. In most cases, you do not want the flag to "wave" while you are painting brush strokes.

Practice your strokes on a sheet of acetate laid right over the worksheets.

Stroke Worksheet

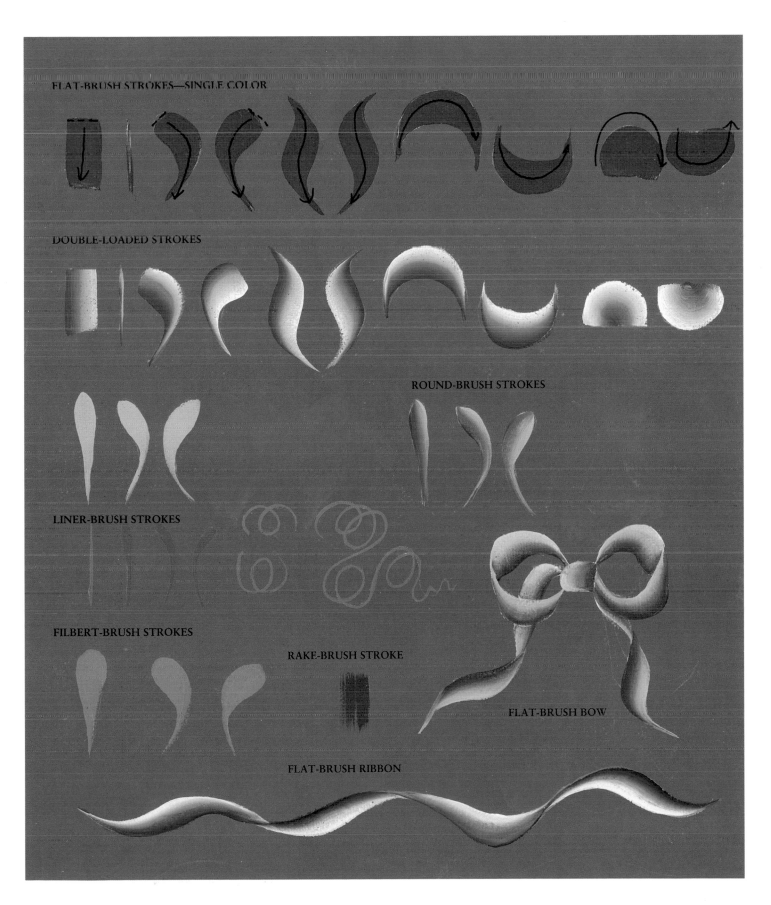

FLAT-BRUSH STROKES—SINGLE COLOR

DOUBLE-LOADED STROKES

ROUND-BRUSH STROKES

LINER-BRUSH STROKES

FILBERT-BRUSH STROKES

RAKE-BRUSH STROKE

FLAT-BRUSH BOW

FLAT-BRUSH RIBBON

Double-Loading

Double-loading means to carry two colors side by side on the brush at the same time, with the colors gradually blending into each other where they meet in the middle. Double-loading with a round brush is done in the same way that we double-load the flat brush. It is harder to double-load round brushes because they come to a point, unlike the flat brush, which is easy to divide in half.

It takes practice, patience and careful attention to learn how to properly double-load a brush. Can you paint without learning to double-load? Yes, but not very well, not beautifully, quickly, or easily. Double-loading techniques enable you to do so many things. Trust me and pay your dues. Practice double-loading!

1. First set up your palette. Squeeze two desired colors, such as a dark and light green, onto your palette. Mix each color to a thin-creamy consistency. Push each color into a neat little pile with your palette knife so that each

has a good clean edge to double-load against.

Put light pressure on the brush to spread the hairs and stroke up against the edge of the lightest color fifteen or twenty times. Approximately half of the brush will be in the light color and half of the brush on the clean palette.

2. With the clean side of the brush, stroke up against the edge of the dark color. Be careful not to push in too far. Stroke many times, as you want the hairs of the brush to fill with paint.

3. To really get the brush full of paint, it is necessary to blend on the palette to soften the color. Do this by stroking the brush back and forth in one spot so the two colors will blend into each other in the middle of the brush. Be careful not to flip the brush or let the light side stray into the darker paint. Then go back and pick up more paint. Your brush must be full. You don't want a space between the two colors in the center of the brush—you want them to blend, one into the other,

in the center.

4. Blend on one side of the brush, then turn the brush over and blend on the other side. This pushes the paint through the hairs of the brush from front to back. Keep the dark color in the center, as shown in the photograph, and when refilling the brush, always blend in the same spot on the palette so you won't be losing all the paint from your brush.

Load the lightest side first.

Stroke the opposite side of the brush repeatedly through the darker color.

Blend on palette to soften.

The top brushstroke was made with a brush that has been properly blended to soften the colors. The lower stroke was not blended properly, leaving a stark transition between the two colors.

When blending on palette, always stroke in the same spot.

This is how your brush should look when properly double-loaded.

Floating

Floating means to fill the brush with painting and blending medium or water on one side and color on the other side, then blend on the palette to soften the color. Shadows or highlights may be applied by floating in two different ways.

The first way is to fill the brush with water, blot it on a rag, then double-load the brush with the color on one side and water on the other. Blend on the palette to soften the color so that it graduates beautifully in the brush from dark to medium to water. Then apply the float in the proper area.

The second way is to double-load the brush with painting and blending medium and color. The painting and blending medium is thicker in consistency than the water and is sometimes easier for the beginner to handle. The paint is applied to the brush and blended in the same way. The color is then floated on the surface. Since acrylics dry so fast, the key to a successful float is:

1. the proper consistency of paint,
2. the proper fill of the brush,
3. blending on palette to soften colors before the shading is done.

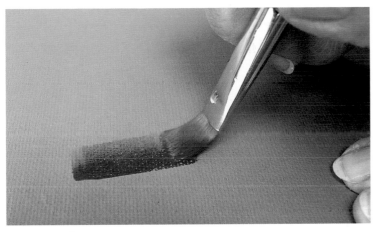

Floating with water.

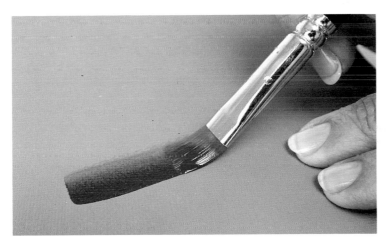

Floating with blending medium.

Applying an Anchor

Applying an anchor means to float a dark shading color, shadow or highlight over a basecoated subject. The anchor is allowed to dry completely, and then the painting technique is applied over the top of the dried anchor and/or highlight. This technique is usually used with acrylics.

Because of the transparency of acrylics, often the shadows move around too much when blended. By applying an anchor before blending begins, this problem is eliminated. A good example of an anchor would be the shadows on this poppy petal.

1. First you would base-coat the poppy and allow it to dry.

2. Next, double-load the brush with water and the shading color and blend on your palette to soften the color.

3. Float the anchor and let it dry.

4. Finally, set up the poppy petal and blend. Because the anchor is floated and dried, it will not move when the blending is executed.

Here the anchor is being applied.

Blending

Essentially, blending is the combination of two or more colors. It is usually done with flat brushes and thick paint the consistency of cake icing or soft butter. Because stroking requires a flowing paint consistency, the skills required for blending are entirely different.

It is essential that when you learn to blend, you use a very light touch. When I first tried this technique, I wanted to press down on the painting, which of course, creates an overblended, muddy mess. With practice, you will learn to barely touch the hairs of your brush to the paint, just as a butterfly's wing would feel if it brushed the side of your face.

Beginners often find blending with acrylics difficult, because they do not have the skills and techniques committed to memory, and therefore work too slowly. Remember that when painting with acrylics, you have to move fast in order to keep them wet enough to blend. This is why I recommend beginners learn to blend first with oils, and then, if desired, move to acrylics once they have become skilled in the technique.

Don't confuse glazing and blending techniques. Glazing, which means to build multiple layers of thinned color on top of each other, is not at all the same as blending two or more colors together.

There are two types of blending that I teach in my seminars. One is simply blending by lightly stroking and cross-blending the paint. The other type of blending, which has been predominately used in this book, is pat blending. Pat blending is the way we paint folds into draped fabrics and ripples into flower petals.

I painted the worksheets in this book on artist's canvas, with the exception of the raw wood worksheet. Using a painted canvas is a very good way for you to practice blending acrylics. The canvas actually has little hills and valleys in it, so that when you put an acrylic extender or blending medium down, the hills and valleys act like little cups and hold the extender, giving you more time to blend.

DIRECTIONAL STROKE BLENDING

Directional blending means to blend following the natural curve or direction that a leaf or flower grows. For example, we blend a leaf from the base out into its strokes, following the movement of the leaf. Then we lightly blend back from the tip of the leaf, along the edges toward the base or bottom of the leaf, following the same direction.

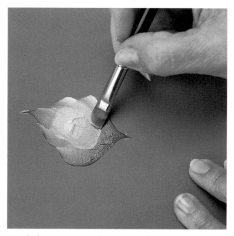

Lightly merge colors together.

Lightly blend from the base out into each of the five strokes.

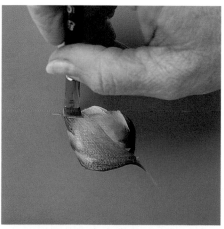

Stroke back toward base of leaf. Lightly blend from the base out into each of the five strokes.

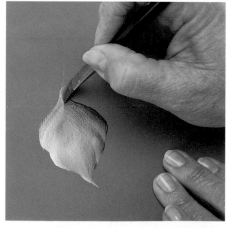

Continue blending not only from the base out, but from the outside edge of each stroke back toward the base.

PAT BLENDING

When we pat blend, we move the colors together in a different way than when we stroke blend. Pat blending moves the paint sideways in dark and light streaks. The streaks themselves, away from the painting, can almost resemble little tornadoes. It is a more sophisticated technique than directional blending, and can eventually lead the artist to produce photorealistic images.

When pat blending is completed, a mop-type brush can be used to eliminate the brushstrokes, but not the shadows or highlights. Learning to pat blend takes more time and patience than stroke blending. It requires plenty of thick paint and the use of as large a brush as possible. The brush should be held high on the handle so the surface of the brush can be flat on the subject that is being blended. A relatively light touch is used when handling the paint.

The only way to learn to pat blend is to practice, practice, practice. In the photographs and on the step-by-step color worksheets in both the leaves and flower chapters, I have tried to illustrate to the best of my ability the technique of pat blending. See the tips on page 118 (pansy demo).

Notice how the pat blending moves the color sideways. Use as large a brush as possible when pat blending.

ACRYLIC BLENDING ON RAW WOOD

The previous blending techniques are meant for use on a painted or stained surface. If you wish to blend on unfinished wood, the technique is a little different.

1. First, neatly transfer your design to the sanded raw wood. Apply a generous amount of blending and painting medium (one that is not too thin—you don't want it to bleed) to your design area.

2. Now apply a good amount of acrylic paint to the wood that has been wet with medium.

3. Blend as desired. As long as the wood stays wet with medium, the acrylics will also stay wet. This gives you ample time to blend, shade, highlight and move the color around.

I recommend practicing this technique on a scrap piece of raw wood first as each type of raw wood will perform differently. If your extender should bleed past the edges of your pattern, carefully enlarge your design to cover the bleed.

Apply blending medium.

Apply acrylics over wet areas.

Blend.

OVERBLENDING

Overblending makes mud. It can be caused by applying too much pressure on the brush, paint that is too thin, or simply blending too long or wiping too much paint off of the surface you are painting. When painting, you have to learn when to stop. This comes with practice. You should stop blending when your subject looks good to you and while you can still see all of the colors that you have applied.

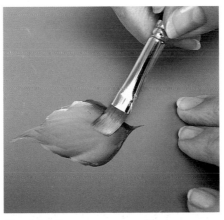

Overblending creates a muddy mess.

4

Leaves

L eaves are every painter's dilemma, but once you've really learned how to paint them, you'll love to do it. After all, there is hardly a flower that blooms without leaves, so if you're going to paint flowers, you'll need to learn to paint leaves as well. There are as many different types of leaves to paint as there are beautiful flowers. By varying my techniques, you will find that you are able to create any type of leaf you desire.

Mixing Greens

In the world of decorative painting, we do not work with an established light source, because we are painting perhaps over the top or around a piece of furniture or other decorative object. Therefore, we say that what is the closest to us will be the lightest, what is in the middle will be the medium value, and what appears to be the furthest away will be the darkest. Before you begin to paint any design on an item, study your master pattern or design and establish which leaves will be the dark, medium and light.

To paint these three values, you will need three colors of green for painting leaves. If you are using acrylics, look for Hauser Dark, Medium and Light Greens. These lovely colors have been pre-mixed for you. However, I want you to know how to mix these colors whether you are working in oils or acrylics.

MEDIUM GREEN
I begin by mixing what I call the mother green. I add a touch of Lamp Black to Cadmium Yellow Medium. This creates a lovely medium-value green.

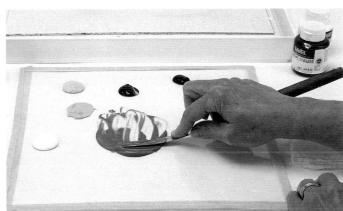

DARK GREEN
Take a portion of the medium green and add a lot of black to it. This will give you a very dark green.

LIGHT GREEN

Take another portion of the medium green and add Cadmium Yellow Light and just a little white. This will give you a light-value green. You will notice that these three greens are yellow-greens.

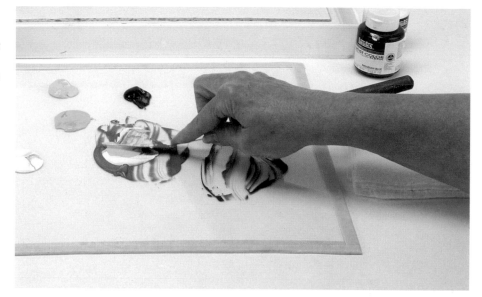

HAUSER BLUE-GREENS

To create the Hauser or blue-greens, add a touch of Prussian Blue to each of the greens above. Now you have the equivalent of the Hauser or blue-green mixes.

The Basic Brushstroke, Dry-Brush Blended Leaf

Because I feel the combinations of techniques for this leaf are so important, I have created worksheets in both oils and acrylics for you to compare. You will notice that really the only difference is the fact that when using oils, basecoating before painting is generally not necessary. This is because the oils are much more opaque than the acrylics.

I think you will find it easier to learn to paint with the oils, because they are forgiving and do not dry as quickly, allowing you the time you need to learn this technique. Because of the additional steps needed when painting with acrylics, the following step-by-step demonstration is done in acrylics. If painting with oils, skip steps one

through eight of this demonstration.

You may find that acrylics dry very, very fast when trying to stroke and blend, and this may trouble you. Do not despair. Be sure that you have practiced strokes and blending and that you have developed your skills before attempting to make a perfect leaf. If you still have trouble, I highly urge you to practice in oils until you have conquered the technique. Then you will find painting this leaf in acrylic very easy to do.

Colors Needed
You will notice on the oil worksheet I have shown you a dark leaf and a light leaf. For the dark leaf, I have used

Hauser Green Dark and Burnt Umber for the dark side and the shadow, and Hauser Green Dark and Ice Blue for the light side of the leaf. Colors in the center of the dark leaf are Hauser Green Light and Ice Blue.

For the light leaf, use Hauser Green Light and a little Burnt Umber for the dark side and shadow. Hauser Green Light and white are used on the light side. Colors in the center of the light leaf are Cadmium Yellow Light and white. (Other colors may be blended into the leaf, if desired.)

1. *Acrylics are transparent; therefore, when painting with acrylics, a neat and smooth basecoat will be needed to cover the surface. Sometimes, it takes two or three coats to achieve the proper opacity. For this leaf the basecoating must be done using strokes. Fill a no. 10 flat brush with Hauser Green Light. Paint the first stroke, as shown in the photo.*

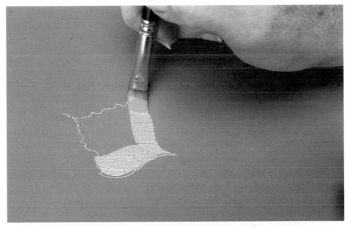

2. *Paint a stroke opposite the first stroke, as shown in the photo.*

3. *Paint a second stroke above the first stroke.*

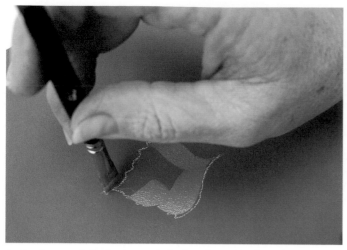

4. At the tip of the leaf, stand the brush on the flat edge.

5. Pull and let the brush roll to the left, creating an incomplete S-stroke.

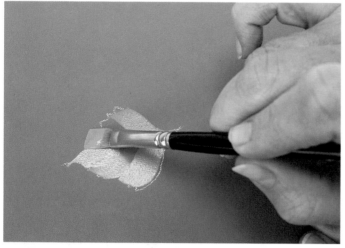

6. Pull a stroke on the opposite side, across from your third stroke.

7. Fill in the center and let dry.

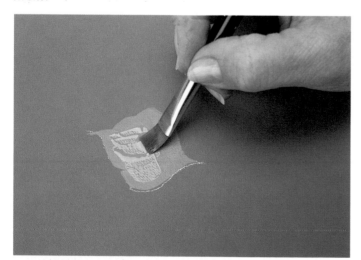

8. Apply a little painting and blending medium to the basecoated leaf. This completes the basecoating section. From here on the steps are much the same for oils or acrylics.

9. Double-load a no. 10 flat brush with Hauser Green Medium and Burnt Umber. Blend on the palette to soften the color. If you wish to use a tiny touch of Prussian Blue mixed with the Burnt Umber, you may do so. Or you may choose to use the Hauser Green Dark for the deepest shading color. Apply the shadow, as shown in the photo.

10. With the double-loaded brush, the first stroke pulls into the shadow. You will notice that this step looks the same as the last, but a basic brushstroke, dry-brush blended leaf has only five strokes. The shadow is not counted as one of these strokes.

11. Place a second stroke above the first stroke. Notice the Burnt Umber side of the double-loaded brush stays to the outside or bottom of the stroke.

12. Refill the brush, if necessary. Stand the brush on the flat edge, the Burnt Umber pointing up.

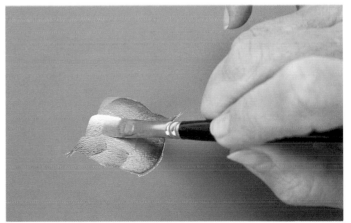

13. Pull and roll the brush to the left, creating an incomplete S-stroke.

14. Wipe the brush and fill it with Hauser Green Medium and white. Quickly blend on the palette to soften the color. Place the fourth stroke opposite stroke number two.

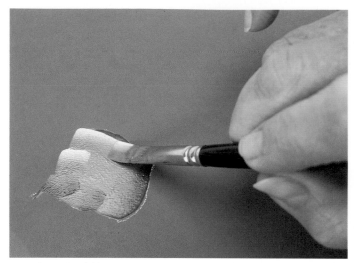

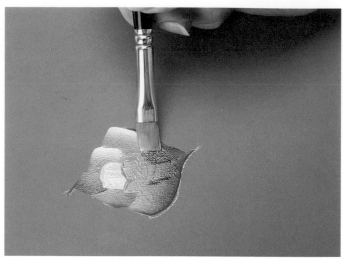

15. *Place the fifth stroke opposite stroke number one.*

16. *Wipe brush and pick up a generous amount of Cadmium Yellow Medium. Apply this in the center of the leaf. Next pick up a little Hauser Green Light and a touch of Hauser Green Dark. Apply these colors under the yellow.*

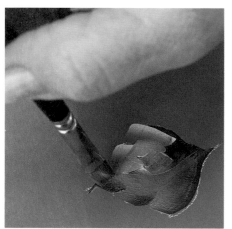

17. *Lightly merge the colors together, then begin to directional blend, lightly stroking from the base out toward each of the five strokes.*

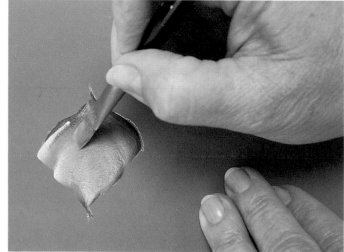

18. *Wipe the brush and lightly pull from the outside edges back toward the base or bottom of the leaf. Turn your canvas as you work so you are painting in a comfortable position.*

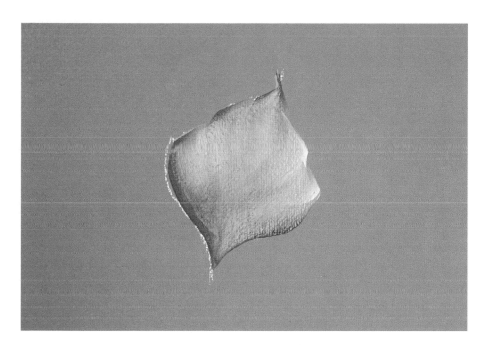

19. *Your leaf should look like this when you have finished the directional blending. If directional blending is properly done as illustrated on the worksheet, your blending will automatically flow in the direction the leaf is growing. If contrast is needed on the dark side, pick up a tiny touch of Ice Blue and accent the outside edges of the strokes by touching, pulling and lifting. Use a very light touch.*

20. *You may paint the vein using thin paint and the point of your liner brush, or you may use a double-loaded comma-like stroke as I did here, which will give a more shaded look.*

21. *Here I have painted both types of veins next to the leaf so you can see the difference in techniques.*

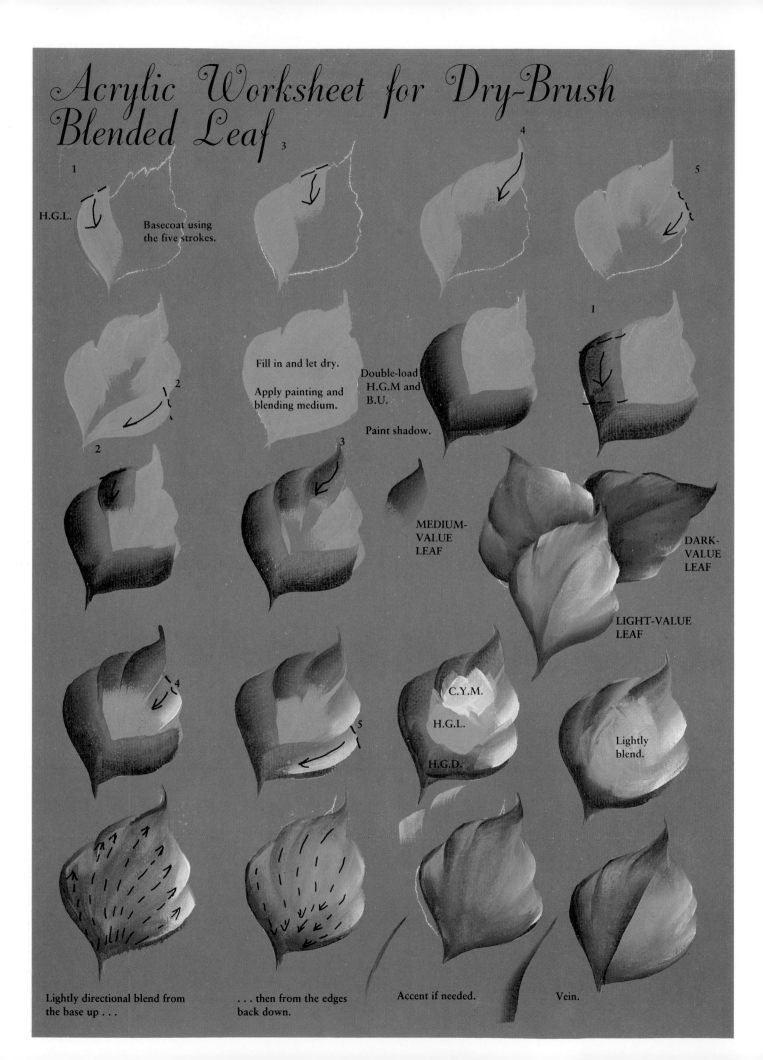

Acrylic Worksheet for Dry-Brush Blended Leaf

1

H.G.L.

Basecoat using the five strokes.

3

4

5

2

Fill in and let dry.

Apply painting and blending medium.

Double-load H.G.M and B.U.

Paint shadow.

1

2

3

MEDIUM-VALUE LEAF

DARK-VALUE LEAF

LIGHT-VALUE LEAF

4

5

C.Y.M.

H.G.L.

H.G.D.

Lightly blend.

Lightly directional blend from the base up . . .

. . . then from the edges back down.

Accent if needed.

Vein.

Oil Worksheet for Dry-Brush Blended Leaf

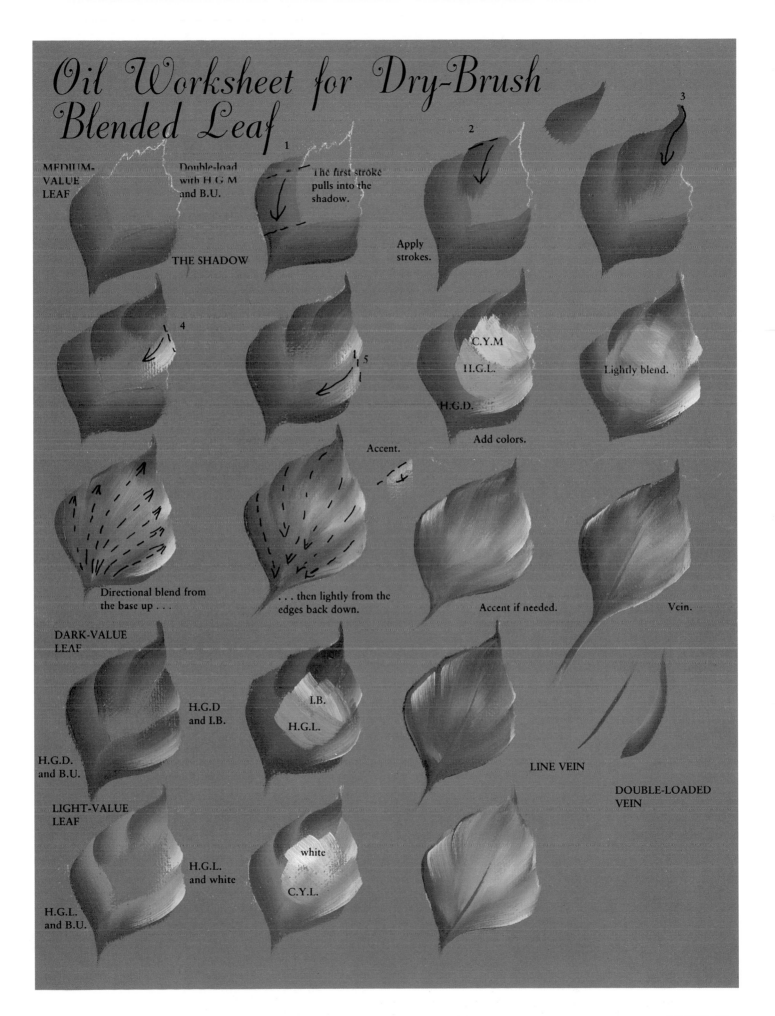

MEDIUM-VALUE LEAF

Double-load with H.G.M and B.U.

THE SHADOW

1 The first stroke pulls into the shadow.

2 Apply strokes.

3

4

5 Accent.

C.Y.M
H.G.L.
H.G.D.
Add colors.

Lightly blend.

Directional blend from the base up . . .

. . . then lightly from the edges back down.

Accent if needed.

Vein.

DARK-VALUE LEAF

H.G.D and I.B.

I.B.
H.G.L.

LINE VEIN

H.G.D. and B.U.

DOUBLE-LOADED VEIN

LIGHT-VALUE LEAF

H.G.L. and white

white
C.Y.L.

H.G.L. and B.U.

Turned Leaves

Creating leaves that turn under and fold over themselves suggests movement in your painting. The first example will show a leaf with the dark side turned and the second with the light side turned.

The following worksheets and demonstrations have all been painted in acrylics. But remember, if you are using oils, undercoating is generally not needed. You simply begin by double-loading the brush and stroking, as directed.

Colors Needed
Hauser Green Medium, Burnt Umber, Titanium White, Cadmium Yellow Medium, Hauser Green Light and Ice Blue.

LEAF WITH DARK EDGE TURNED

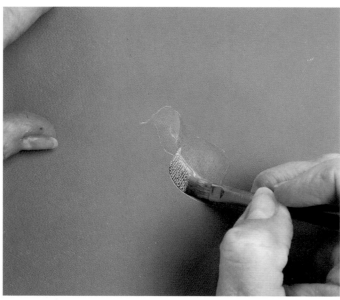

1. Fill a no. 10 flat brush with Hauser Green Medium. Apply the brushstrokes, as shown in the photo. This will let you use brushstrokes to base in the leaves. Let dry and apply a second or even a third coat, as needed, to cover. Now double-load the brush with Hauser Green Medium and Burnt Umber. Blend on palette to soften color. Apply the shadow to the base of the leaf.

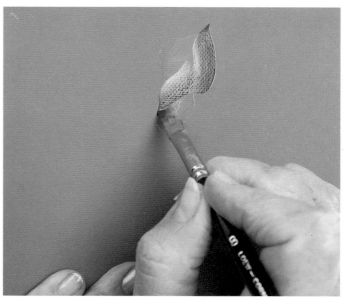

2. Apply strokes 1 and 2, as shown in the photo. I have turned the canvas upside down to apply these strokes. For the third stroke, use an S-type stroke to lead into the turn.

Tip

Turned leaves take a great deal of practice. It will help you immensely if you will practice your strokes right on top of mine, even if you aren't using paint. Simply use a dry brush and follow the strokes until you are comfortable reaching for the angles that make the leaves turn.

3. If it feels better to use a smaller brush for this third stroke, then double-load a no. 6 or no. 8 flat brush with Hauser Green Medium and Burnt Umber. Stand the brush on the flat edge and paint an S-stroke. Notice how the leaf turns.

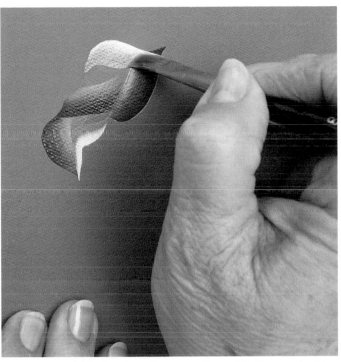

4. Double-load the brush with Hauser Green Medium and white, and apply the strokes on the light side of the turned portion of the leaf.

5. Double-load the brush with Hauser Green Medium and white, and paint the stroke on the light side of the leaf.

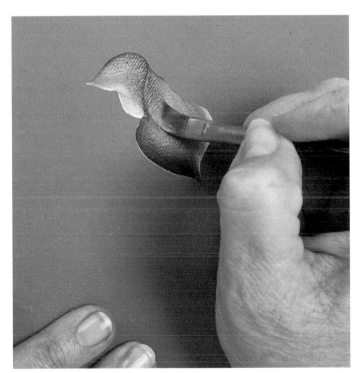

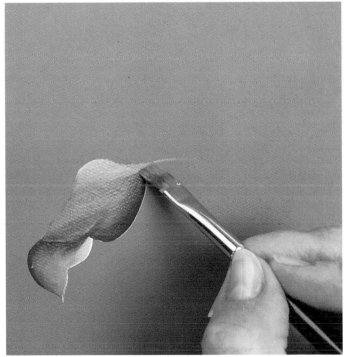

6. Add Hauser Green Light and Cadmium Yellow Medium to the center of the leaf. Quickly wipe the brush and blend the colors together. Stroke from the base of the leaf out toward the edges and then from the outside edge back toward the base.

7. Accent the edges of the leaf, using Ice Blue, if needed.

LEAF WITH LIGHT EDGE TURNED

1. *Basecoat the leaf using brushstrokes. Let dry. Double-load the brush with Hauser Green Medium and Burnt Umber. Blend on the palette to soften color. Apply the shadow and the first stroke as shown in the photo.*

2. *Apply the second stroke above the first.*

3. *For the third stroke, create an incomplete S-stroke at the tip of the leaf.*

4. Now double-load with Hauser Green Medium and white. Follow my stroke directions in the photos and on the worksheet to paint the turned light side of the leaf. I apply three strokes to make the leaf turn.

5. Fill in the center with Cadmium Yellow Medium and Hauser Green Light. Lightly blend. Accent the edge with two little comma-like strokes. This breaks the edge of the leaf and makes it look more like the stroked side. Vein using the liner brush or the flat edge of the flat brush with thin Burnt Umber as shown on the worksheet. You will notice that I have placed a tiny highlight of white next to the Burnt Umber. This may be done, if you desire.

Turned Leaf Worksheet

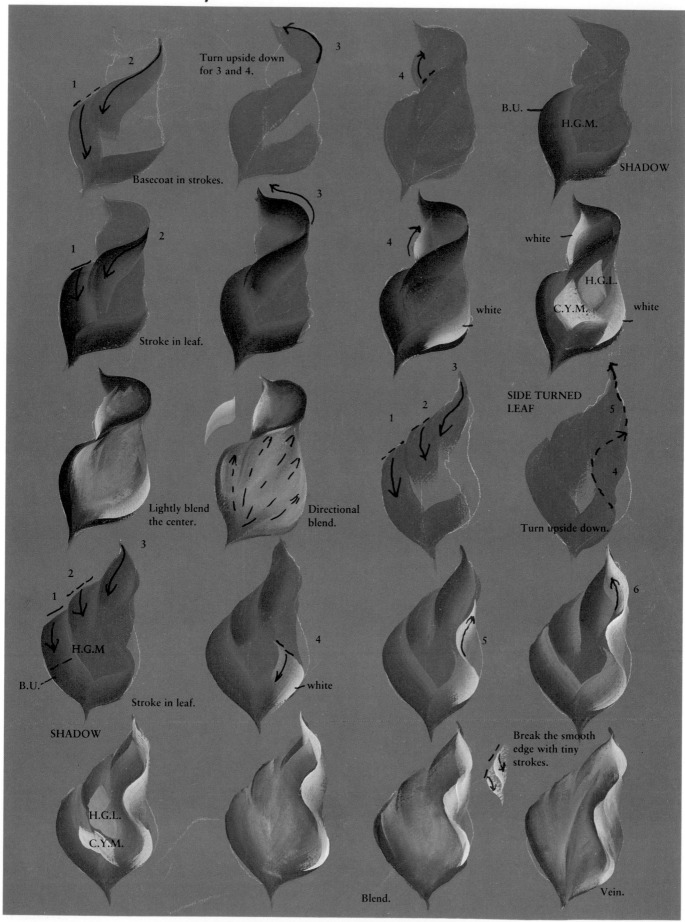

Turn upside down for 3 and 4.

Basecoat in strokes.

B.U.

H.G.M.

SHADOW

white

Stroke in leaf.

white

white

H.G.L.

C.Y.M.

white

SIDE TURNED LEAF

Lightly blend the center.

Directional blend.

Turn upside down.

H.G.M

B.U.

Stroke in leaf.

white

SHADOW

Break the smooth edge with tiny strokes.

H.G.L.

C.Y.M.

Blend.

Vein.

Blade Leaves

Tulip, iris, daffodil and jonquil leaves are what we call blade leaves. These leaves should also be painted, like all other leaves, in dark, medium and light values. As with the last demonstration, the worksheet was painted with acrylics. If using oils, the technique is the same, but generally the basecoating is not necessary.

Colors Needed for a Medium-Value Leaf
Hauser Green Light, Hauser Green Medium, Hauser Green Dark, Burnt Umber, Titanium White, Cadmium Yellow Medium.

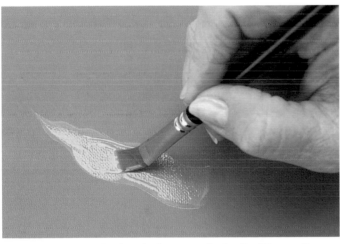

1. Using a no. 10 flat brush, basecoat the leaf in Hauser Green Light or Medium, if you desire. Two or three coats will be needed to cover. Let dry, then apply painting and blending medium to the leaf.

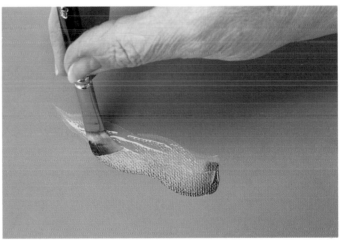

2. Double-load the brush with Hauser Green Medium and Burnt Umber. Blend on the palette to soften the color. Apply the shadow at the base or the shadow point on the leaf and along the dark side.

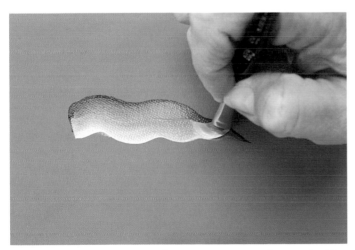

3. Double-load the brush with Hauser Green Medium and white. Blend on palette to soften the color. Stroke along the light side of the leaf with the white to the outside of the brush.

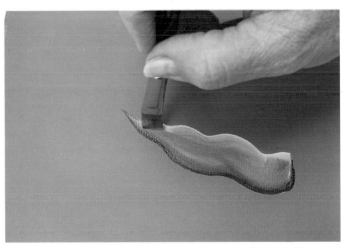

4. Wipe the brush and quickly add Cadmium Yellow Medium and Hauser Green Light to the center. Wipe the brush and blend from the bottom to the top and back, using a light touch. Be sure you use plenty of paint, or the paint will dry so fast you will not be able to achieve the blended effect you desire.

Blade Leaf Worksheet

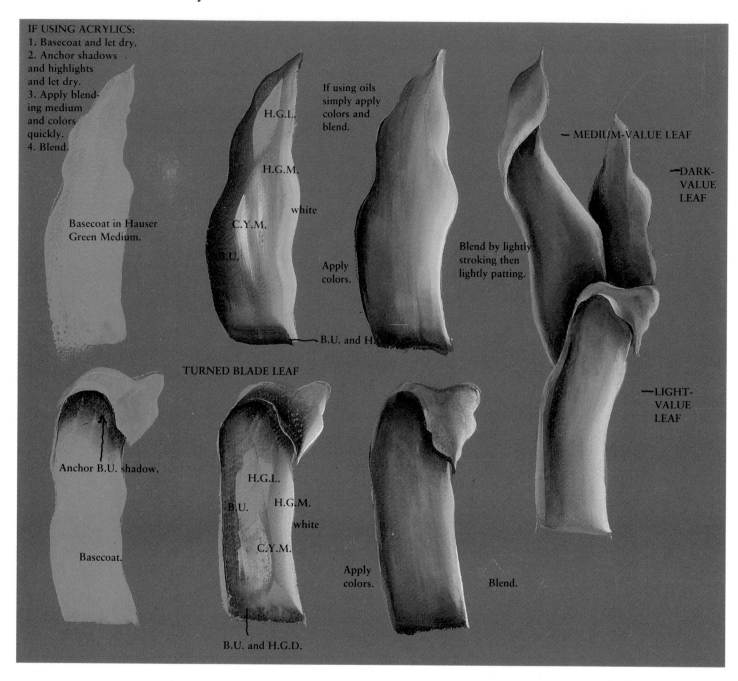

IF USING ACRYLICS:
1. Basecoat and let dry.
2. Anchor shadows and highlights and let dry.
3. Apply blending medium and colors quickly.
4. Blend.

Basecoat in Hauser Green Medium.

H.G.L.

H.G.M.

white

C.Y.M.

B.U.

If using oils simply apply colors and blend.

Apply colors.

B.U. and H.

Blend by lightly stroking then lightly patting.

— MEDIUM-VALUE LEAF

—DARK-VALUE LEAF

—LIGHT-VALUE LEAF

TURNED BLADE LEAF

Anchor B.U. shadow.

Basecoat.

H.G.L.

B.U.

H.G.M.

white

C.Y.M.

B.U. and H.G.D.

Apply colors.

Blend.

The Scribble Leaf

If you can scribble with a pencil, you can paint this leaf. The back and forth motion makes an attractive jagged edged leaf that is lovely to use with a poppy, a Shasta daisy or any of the other flowers that boast jagged-edged leaves.

Remember, this acrylic demonstration will include basecoating; if using oils, skip this step.

Colors Needed for a Medium-Value Leaf

Hauser Green Light, Hauser Green Medium, Hauser Green Dark, Burnt Umber, Titanium White and Cadmium Yellow Medium.

1. To undercoat with acrylics, fill the brush with Hauser Green Light or Medium. Begin to scribble back and forth slowly and neatly, creating the very beautiful, jagged, rough edges of this leaf. On the left side, I usually paint from the bottom up. When I paint the right side, I turn the leaf upside down and scribble slowly, working toward the top of the leaf. Fill in the center and let dry. Apply a second coat of paint, if needed, to cover. Apply painting and blending medium to the center of the leaf. Double-load the brush with Hauser Green Medium and Burnt Umber. Blend on the palette to soften the color. Apply the shadow, then carefully scribble on top of your basecoat scribbles, if working with acrylics, with the Burnt Umber to the outside. If desired, wipe the brush and pick up a little white. Continue scribbling toward the top. This gives a pretty variation to the leaf.

2. *Turn the leaf upside down. Double-load the brush with Hauser Green Medium and white and begin to carefully and neatly scribble, working toward yourself and the tip of the leaf.*

3. *Add the colors of your choice to the center. I used Cadmium Yellow Medium and Hauser Green Light. Apply a little bit of Hauser Green Dark at the bottom of the leaf. Quickly wipe the brush and blend. Add more paint, if needed. Veining may be done by filling a no. 1 liner brush with thin paint. Use the darkest shading color you used on the leaves or double-load a flat brush with the medium green and the darkest shading color. Make a comma-like stroke, as shown on the worksheet, to create a shaded vein.*

Scribble Leaf Worksheet

start

Neatly scribble on basecoat.

start

Turn upside down and scribble toward you.

white or B.U.

Double-load with B.U. and H.G.L.

Double-load with H.G.L. and white.

Scribble colors on edges.

H.G.L.

C.Y.M.

H.G.D.

B.U.

Apply colors.

Blend.

Vein.

H.G.D.

B.U.

5
Flowers

This chapter will teach you to paint dozens of lovely flowers in both oils and acrylics. Each flower demonstration includes step-by-step instructions, worksheets for you to practice on, black-and-white patterns for you to trace and transfer to your practice or project surface, and several beautiful, full-page project ideas showing how you can combine the flowers, leaves and accessories you've learned in this book to decorate an endless variety of surfaces.

Daisies

I will forever and always love to paint and to teach people to paint daisies. They can be painted in a multitude of colors, and can be stroked or blended. Daisies are happy flowers, and once you've learned to paint them, you'll share their pleasure.

On the worksheet at the end of this demonstration I have painted the white and yellow daisies using acrylics. The turquoise daisy is painted using oils. The stroke technique I have used may be executed the same way whether you are using acrylics or oils.

Daisies may be created with flat, round or filbert brushes. Each brush will create a slightly different-shaped petal, as shown at right.

Colors Needed
- White Daisy—Titanium White and Payne's Gray
- Yellow Daisy—Cadmium Yellow Medium and Burnt Sienna
- Turquoise Daisy—Turquoise and Titanium White
- Center Colors for all Daisies—Cadmium Yellow Medium, Burnt Sienna, Burnt Umber and white
- Ribbon—Gold, Burnt Sienna, Cadmium Yellow Light or Cadmium Yellow Medium and white

Tip

If you will divide the daisy into quarters it will be easier to see which direction each brushstroke should angle toward. Do not vary these directions or your daisy will look like a pinwheel instead of a beautiful flower.

Flat-brush petals.

Filbert-brush petals.

Round-brush petals.

WHITE DAISY

1. Fill the brush with relatively thin white paint.

2. You are going to paint a variation of the comma stroke to form the daisy petals. Starting at the outside edge of each petal, touch, press and lift as you pull in toward the center. A second coat of paint may be needed to cover if you are using acrylics. Let dry.

3. Using water or painting medium, float Payne's Gray onto each petal at the center.

4. To paint the center, basecoat in white if using acrylics. Let dry. Next, basecoat in Cadmium Yellow Medium and let dry. Double-load the brush with Cadmium Yellow Medium and Burnt Sienna. Blend on the palette to soften the color. Shade the center with the Burnt Sienna.

5. Double-load the brush with Cadmium Yellow Medium and white. Blend on the palette to soften the color. Highlight the center with white.

6. The dots are applied with the point of a good liner brush. Don't line them up like mouse tracks—let them be loose and free. Their main function is to join the center with the petals. I paint dots of Burnt Umber first, then scatter a few dots of white. If desired, touches of other colors, such as yellow, green or even a few dots of Cadmium Red Light may be used.

TURQUOISE DAISY

1. Basecoat in turquoise.

2. Overstroke with white whipped with turp to the consistency of whipped cream. You will notice on the turquoise daisy, I deliberately double-stroked each petal with white to give it a different look. You may use double strokes or single strokes. Either creates a lovely daisy.

Tip

Remember, when using acrylics, you want to paint the overstrokes before the undercoat color has dried. This is what will give you the beautiful shading.

Daisy and Ribbon Worksheet

SINGLE STROKE DAISY

Stroke petals in white or color of choice.
A second coat may be needed.

Shade with P.G. or color of choice.

Stroke in C.Y.M.

CENTERS

Basecoat in white if
needed to cover.

Shade with B.S.

Highlight if desired
with white.

C.Y.M.

C.Y.M.

Shade with B.S.

B.S.

Dots should be
a bit loose.

DOUBLE-STROKE DAISY

Turquoise

Double-stroke petals in white.

RIBBON

Gold

Shade with B.S.

C.Y.L. or C.Y.M.   Shade with B.S.

Highlight with white.

Pattern for top of candle box.

Pattern for front of wheelbarrow.

Pattern for side of wheelbarrow.

These patterns may be photocopied for personal use.
Enlarge at 143 percent to return to full size.

"IN A COUNTRY GARDEN"
I found this darling little wheelbarrow at a
flea market. I cleaned it as described on
page 20, and then painted over its original
finish.

"A SPRING BOUQUET"
This wooden candle box is manufactured
by Walnut Hollow. After sanding it and
wiping with a tack rag, I painted it turquoise and added a garden of daisies.

Geraniums, Lilacs and Other Stroke Flowers

Geraniums, lilacs and other flowers that grow in clumps are most easily painted using brushstrokes. They are magnificent in both oils and acrylics. The key to painting these flowers is:

1. Contrast—flowers that are to the back or in the shadow are much darker than those on the top.

2. Uneven edges—so they don't look like a snowball.

3. Loose and airy feeling—rather than a solid mass of flower.

Carefully study these flowers on the following step-by-step worksheet. Then give them a try. The brush size you use will depend upon the size of the flowers you are painting. I did not include individual projects for these flowers.

Colors Needed

- Geranium Petals—Burgundy, Cadmium Red Medium, Cadmium Red Light and Cadmium Orange
- Geranium Centers—Cadmium Yellow Light and Lamp Black
- Geranium Leaves—Hauser Green Light, Hauser Green Medium, Hauser Green Dark, Titanium White, Burgundy and Burnt Umber
- Lilacs—Titanium White, Prussian Blue, and Mauve or Dioxazine Purple

Geranium Worksheet

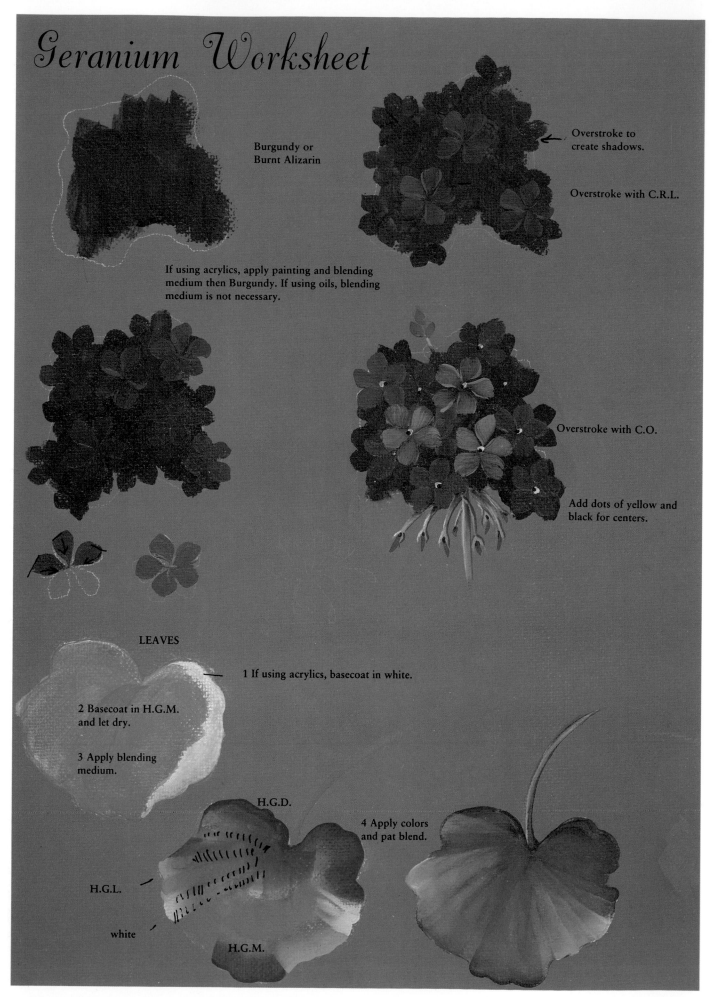

Burgundy or
Burnt Alizarin

Overstroke to
create shadows.

Overstroke with C.R.L.

If using acrylics, apply painting and blending
medium then Burgundy. If using oils, blending
medium is not necessary.

Overstroke with C.O.

Add dots of yellow and
black for centers.

LEAVES

1 If using acrylics, basecoat in white.

2 Basecoat in H.G.M.
and let dry.

3 Apply blending
medium.

H.G.D.

4 Apply colors
and pat blend.

H.G.L.

white

H.G.M.

Lilac Worksheet

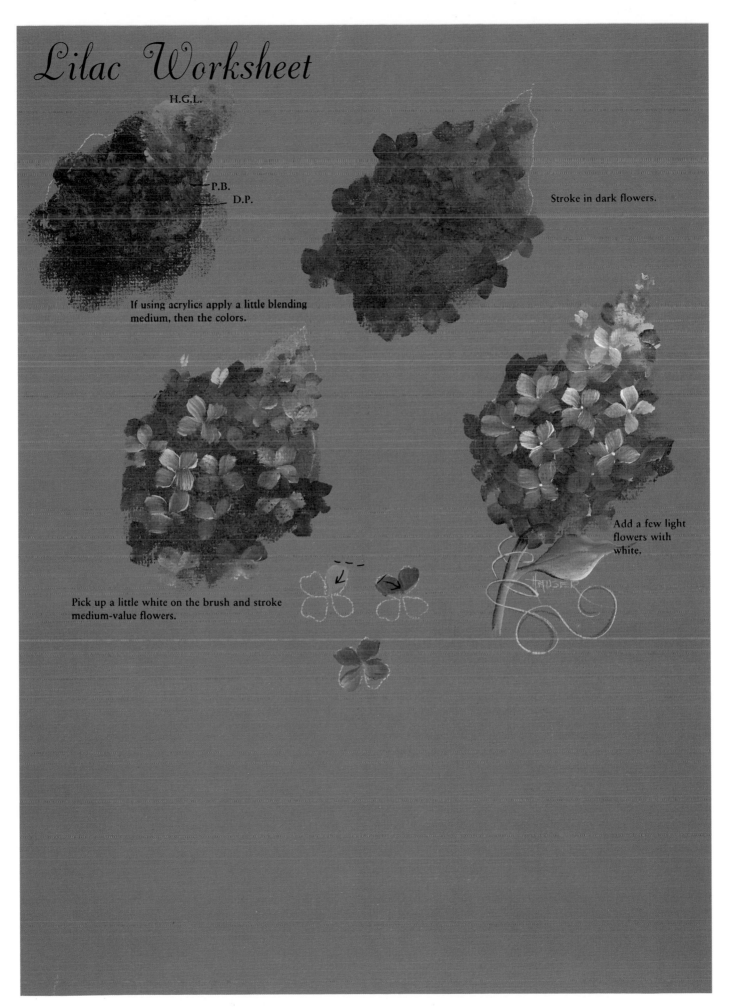

H.G.L.

P.B.

D.P.

If using acrylics apply a little blending medium, then the colors.

Stroke in dark flowers.

Pick up a little white on the brush and stroke medium-value flowers.

Add a few light flowers with white.

Violets

The dainty little violet was my mother's favorite flower. Whether painted singularly or in bunches, their delicate, feminine charm leaves an everlasting trail of beauty. The technique is the same, whether using acrylics or oils.

Colors Needed
- Violet petals—Dioxazine Purple, Titanium White, Cadmium Yellow Light and Cadmium Red Light
- Violet calyxes and stems—Hauser Green Medium or Hauser Green Light, Burnt Umber and white

1. The size of the brush will depend upon the size of the violet you are painting. On the worksheet, I used a no. 4 flat brush. Stroke in a little Dioxazine Purple and then stroke in white until you have achieved the desired color. Paint the back two petals first, using comma strokes. Start at the outside edge and pull and lift in toward the center. The two side strokes come next.

2. To create the lead petal, which is the largest petal, paint a stroke in the center and then a stroke on each side, as shown on the worksheet. This will take some practice, but if you will look carefully, you will notice that the lead petal almost forms a heart. Let the petals dry.

3. To shade the darker center, float on Dioxazine Purple. When stroking the violets in oils, it usually isn't necessary to go back and shade deeper at the center. As shown on the worksheet, the center of the violet is V-shaped. Using a very fine liner brush, paint two comma-like strokes. Be sure you connect all five petals, as shown on the worksheet. The points of the comma strokes actually open out onto the lead petal. Carefully fill the center with a little Cadmium Yellow Light. Then add a tiny dot of Cadmium Red Light.

The calyxes are painted in Hauser Green Medium or Hauser Green Light. Shade dark areas with Burnt Umber and highlight with white. Be sure the stems and calyxes are very neatly and daintily done. Use an excellent liner brush for the stem and a very small flat brush to form the calyxes.

Violet Worksheet

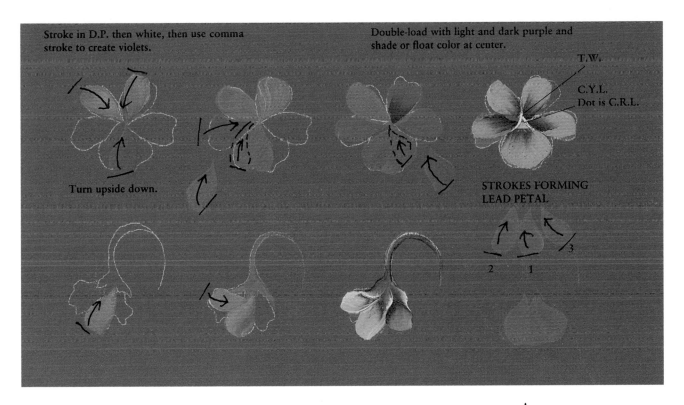

Stroke in D.P. then white, then use comma stroke to create violets.

Turn upside down.

Double-load with light and dark purple and shade or float color at center.

T.W.

C.Y.L.

Dot is C.R.L.

STROKES FORMING
LEAD PETAL

3
2   1

Pattern for top of box.
*These patterns may be photocopied for personal use.
Enlarge at 200 percent to return to full size.*

Pattern for "From God's Garden.

Border for box.

"A TOUCH OF SPRING"
This little wooden box, by Walnut Hollow,
was first stained white. The design was
then painted onto the unsealed surface.
Basswood is a great raw wood because it's
a little porous, and acrylics blend beauti-
fully on this surface.

"FROM GOD'S GARDEN"
*This gentle piece was painted on an un-
sealed Walnut Hollow raw wood round.
See chapter three for instructions on blending on raw wood. A raw wood worksheet
is shown on page 120.*

Roses

To me, there is no flower more beautiful than a rose. My roses are dedicated to my beloved husband, Jerry. He has put up with my fabulous career, raised our four children, cooked endless meals and supported my enthusiasm and my artistic temperament with rarely a cross word. He has always filled my life with roses. You can fill your life and those of all you love with roses as well. It only takes the knowledge of brushstrokes and double-loading, and the desire to learn how to put them together.

Once a woman watched me paint a rose and said to me, "You painted that rose in less than two minutes. How can you sell these paintings for several hundred dollars, when it takes you such a short time to paint them?" I turned to her, smiled and said, "Yes, two minutes and a lifetime." I didn't have a teacher teach me how to do this, I had to learn myself. Now, it's all laid out for you, step by step. So, if you want to paint roses, get busy!

The following photo demonstration of the pink rose is painted in acrylics. The same steps are used for oils, except you won't need to basecoat. The worksheets are painted in oils. Remember when painting the white rose that a white flower can reflect any color or combination of colors you desire.

Colors Needed
- The Pink Rose—Titanium White and Burgundy
- The Red Rose—Cadmium Red Light and Burnt Alizarin
- The Yellow Rose—Cadmium Yellow Medium, Burnt Sienna, Cadmium Yellow Light, Titanium White and Cadmium Red Light
- The White Rose—Titanium White, Raw Umber, Mauve, Prussian Blue, Burnt Alizarin and Hauser Green Light
- Calyxes, rose hips and stems— Hauser Green Light, Hauser Green Dark, Burnt Umber and Titanium White

1. Remember, when painting with oils, it is generally not necessary to undercoat, as oils are opaque enough to cover. However, with acrylics, undercoating is necessary. First apply some painting and blending medium—I like to try to keep the acrylics wet as much as possible, for the shading is far more beautiful working wet into wet. Then basecoat the design area with Burgundy. The size of the brush you use will depend on the size of the flower you want to paint. On the worksheet I used a no. 8 flat brush. Mix a little Burgundy, or a deep, rich shading red into white. Double-load the brush with this mixed color and straight Burgundy so that it is full of paint. Blend on the palette to soften the color. Apply a scallop stroke at the top of the rose—this is the first of thirteen strokes it will take to do the first half of the rose.

2. Apply a scallop-like comma to the right of stroke 1.

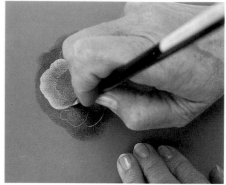

3. Apply a scalloped comma to the left of stroke 1. If you are left-handed, simply reverse this procedure.

4. Pick up a little white on the light side of the brush so there is contrast between the first row and second row of petals. Paint stroke 4 so that it falls between strokes 1 and 3, but below and slightly overlapping the first row of strokes.

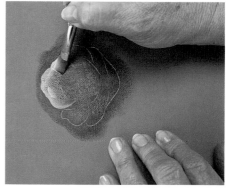

5. Paint another scalloped stroke to the right of stroke 4.

6. Paint a comma stroke at the right edge.

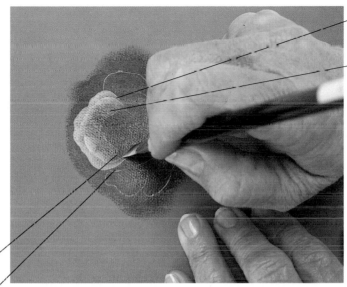

D

C

B

A

7. Paint a comma stroke at the left edge. Make sure the light side of your double-loaded brush is always at the top. Now study your flower. You should see the outside edges or tails of both the back and front rows of strokes. I've labeled these tails or edges A, B, C and D.

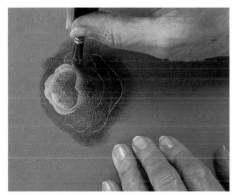

8. Stroke 8 is a scalloped U-stroke connecting the outside edge of B to the outside edge of C. You may go back over this stroke as many times as needed, but keep your double-load clean.

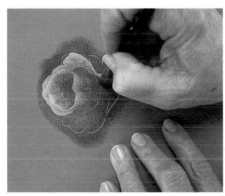

9. Now paint a scalloped comma that starts at D.

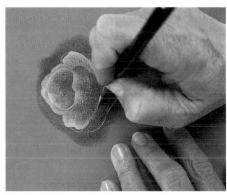

10. Start at A and paint another scalloped comma going in the other direction. Its tail should meet the tail of the comma coming from point D in the center of the rose.

11. *Make another scalloped comma below the first. Its head should start near the center of the first comma, and it should slightly overlap the first comma's tail.*

12. *Repeat the last step on the opposite side. Notice that this comma's tail is pulled below the tail of the previous stroke, rather than joining it in the center.*

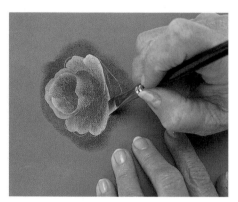

13. *Stroke 13 is an S-stroke that fits in across the bottom. All three steps used in making the S-stroke are shown here. Before proceeding any further, try to learn to paint these first thirteen strokes as perfectly as possible.*

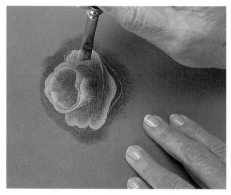

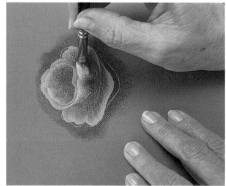

14. *Stroke 14 is another U-stroke that connects tail A to tail D, slightly overlapping your first U-stroke (stroke 8). Sometimes I actually pick my brush up in the middle of this stroke and put it back down to complete a broken stroke.*

15—19. Strokes 15, 16, 17, 18, 19 and so on are over-strokes. They fall on top of the lower strokes. The outside edge of these strokes should be a little lighter in color. I exaggerated this on the color worksheet. Generally, I would not paint these overstrokes with quite as much contrast, but I wanted you to be able to see just exactly what I was doing.

There is no exact set number of these strokes and each rose will turn out a little differently. The most important thing to remember is not to make it look like a tiny rose on top of a large rose. Be sure you reach out far enough to the edge of the under petals with the overstroke.

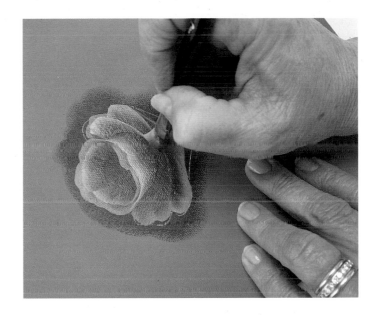

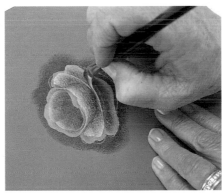

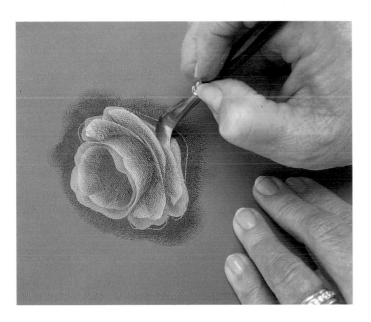

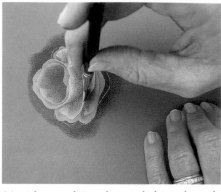  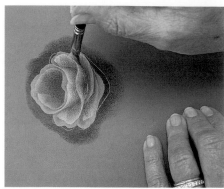

20. *After applying the needed number of fill-in strokes, I will often connect the outside edges of two petals with a rolled S-stroke. This looks like a petal that is cupped up over the center of the flower.*

21. *Here I added a lighter comma stroke to create another fill-in petal.*

22. *To finish the rose, double-load the brush with your light and dark Burgundy mixtures, and carefully paint scallop-like strokes to fill in the center. Be sure you keep them high in the middle and low on the sides—don't paint straight across or you'll create a square and unattractive rose.*

23. Here I've done a "quick fix." My rose looked lopsided at the bottom, so I stroked the bottom petal further to the right, taking it further back under the rose.

Tips

- Be sure you have a high-quality brush in excellent condition.
- Be sure you are well-practiced in brushstrokes and double-loading techniques.
- Be sure you are using the proper consistency of paint: not too thin, but certainly not too thick. This rose is a stroke flower; therefore, the paint must easily flow from the brush.
- It is fine to go back over any stroke as long as you properly hold a double-load.
- Back petals should be darker and petals on top should be a little lighter in order to create contrast.
- Practice the first thirteen strokes until you are comfortable with them, then add the last twenty-one or twenty-two strokes. There is not an exact number of strokes in the last half. They will vary with the size and shape of the strokes you paint.
- Don't be discouraged. Paint your strokes on top of mine one hundred or two hundred times, if necessary, to develop the skill, which will enable you to paint these magnificent flowers.

Rosebuds

Rosebuds can be painted in any combination of colors you desire. They are made up entirely of S-strokes—two that form the bud and then more to create the calyxes around it.

1. If using acrylics, you may wish to undercoat the rosebud with white first. Double-load a flat brush with white and Burgundy. Blend on the palette to soften the color. Paint a U-stroke to form the bottom of the bud. An S-stroke, with the Burgundy to the outside, forms the left side of the bud.

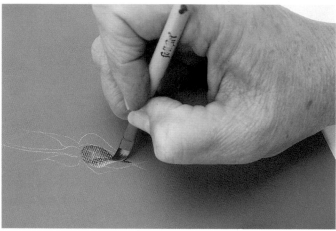

2. Double-load the brush with Burgundy and white. Paint an S-stroke on the opposite side of the rose with the white to the outside.

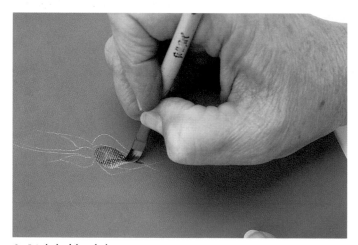

3. Lightly blend the center.

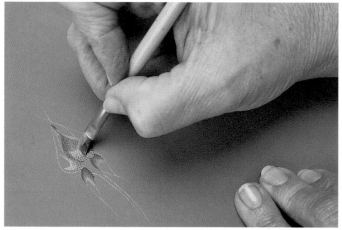

4. To paint the calyxes, double-load the brush with Hauser Green Light and a mixture of Hauser Green Dark plus a touch of Burnt Umber. Blend on the palette to soften the color and paint U-strokes to form the base of the calyxes around the rosebud.

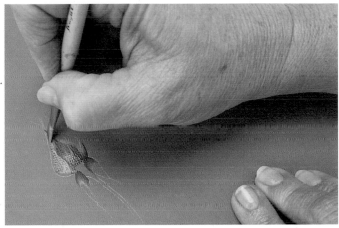

5. Use S-strokes to block in the dark side of each calyx.

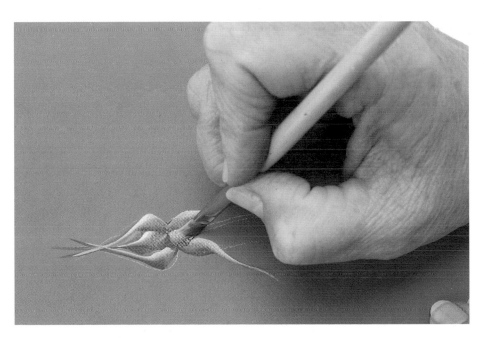

6. Double load the brush with Hauser Green Light and white. Blend on palette to soften the color. Using S strokes, paint the light side of each calyx. Lightly blend in center if needed.

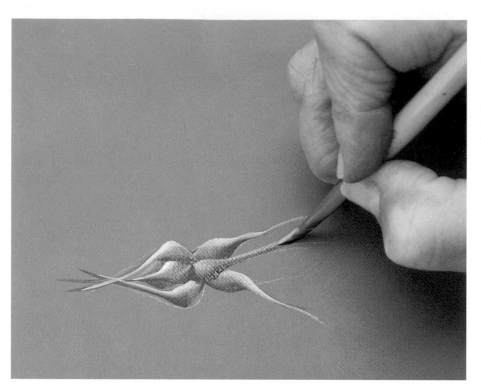

7. The rose hip (the bulb where the base of the flower joins the stem) is painted with a small flat brush using the same color combinations. The stem may be painted with the flat edge of a flat brush or a liner brush, again using the same colors. It is extremely important to shade the stem, in order to achieve a realistic looking rosebud.

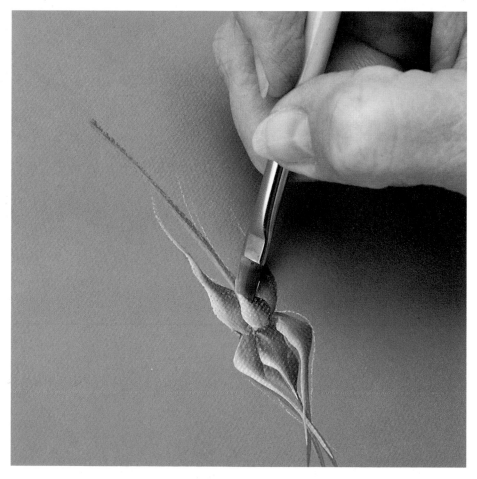

8. Curlicues can be added at random using a liner brush full of very thin paint. The curlicues may be shaded with dark green and highlighted with white, if desired.

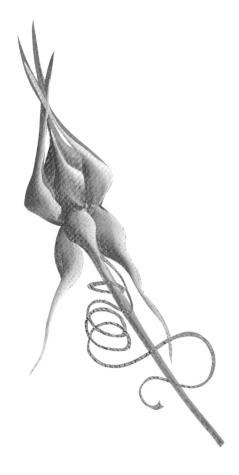

Rose Worksheets

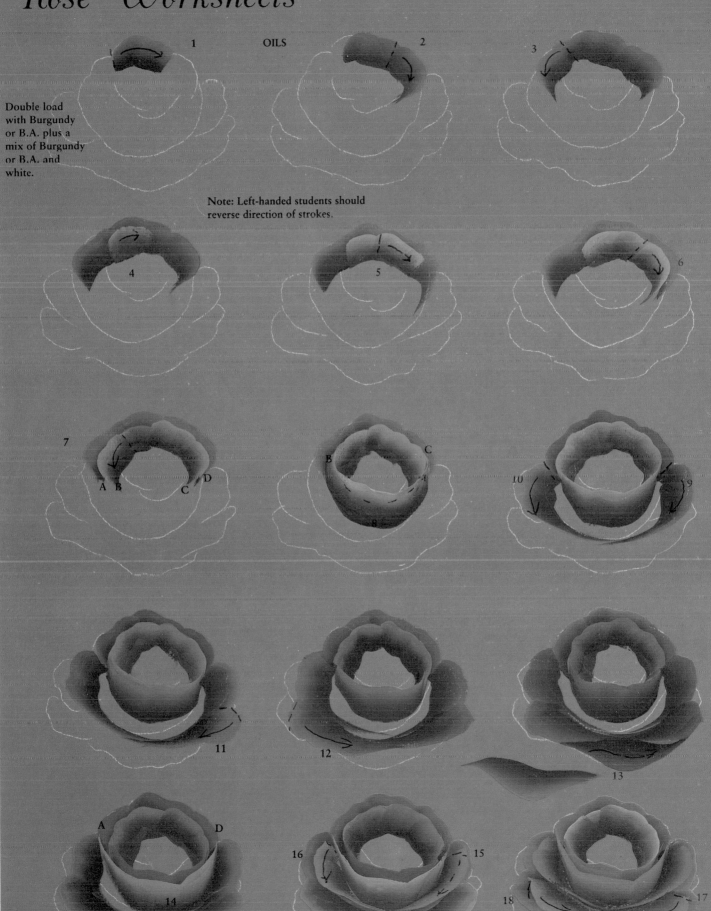

OILS

Double load
with Burgundy
or B.A. plus a
mix of Burgundy
or B.A. and
white.

Note: Left-handed students should
reverse direction of strokes.

REVIEW OF STROKES 15-19

16   15

18   17

19

19   20

THE CENTER   "FILL-IN" PETAL STROKES

ACRYLICS

Apply a small amount   Apply a little Burgundy.
of blending medium.   Stroke rose into wet paint.

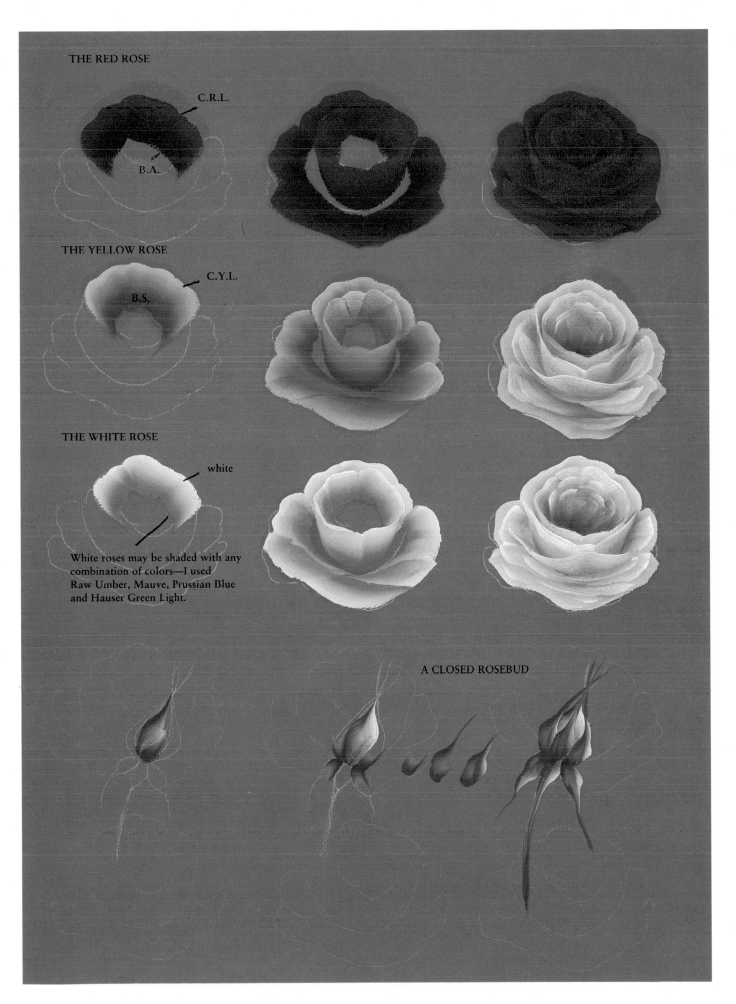

THE RED ROSE

C.R.L.

B.A.

THE YELLOW ROSE

C.Y.L.

B,S,

THE WHITE ROSE

white

White roses may be shaded with any combination of colors—I used Raw Umber, Mauve, Prussian Blue and Hauser Green Light.

A CLOSED ROSEBUD

Pattern for "A Celebration of Roses."

Leaves for front side.

Pattern for "Love Letters." This pattern may be photocopied for personal use. Enlarge at 147 percent to return it to full size.

Pattern for front cluster of roses on carousel horse. This pattern may be photocopied for personal use. Enlarge at 323 percent (or enlarge at 180 percent twice) to return it to full size.

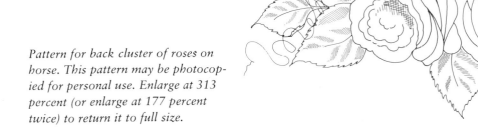

Pattern for back cluster of roses on horse. This pattern may be photocopied for personal use. Enlarge at 313 percent (or enlarge at 177 percent twice) to return it to full size.

**"PENELOPE: A HORSE OF A
DIFFERENT COLOR"**
*This resin horse was first sandblasted, then
basecoated with a gentle off-white and
trimmed in pastel colors.*

"LOVE LETTERS"
To create this elegant keepsake box, paint
the box a slate gray. Let dry. Heavily antique the edges with Payne's Gray and trim
with black.

"A CELEBRATION OF ROSES"
*This garland of roses and ribbon is painted
on a handmade paper filled with rose petals. Such decorative papers may be found
in arts and crafts stores.*

Poppies

I have provided both an oil and an acrylic worksheet for this elegant and colorful flower. The following demonstration is done in acrylics—if you are using oils you won't need to basecoat or float an anchor. Do use plenty of paint. Your oil paint should be the consistency of soft, spreadable butter or cake icing. For the best results, use a very light touch and blend with as large a brush as possible.

Colors Needed
- Red Poppy—Cadmium Red Light, Burgundy or Burnt Alizarin, Cadmium Orange (for acrylics only), Hauser Green Light, Burnt Umber and Titanium White
- White Poppy—Titanium White, Raw Umber, Burnt Alizarin, Mauve and Prussian Blue

Tip

You may reapply paint and paint a petal over, but do not add more extender unless you have let the petal completely dry and cure.

1. Using a no. 6 flat brush, neatly and carefully basecoat the flower. Remember a basecoat should always be as smooth and even as possible. It may take two or more coats to cover. If you are painting on a very dark background, you may first want to neatly undercoat with white. Let this dry and then come back and basecoat with Cadmium Red Light. Anchor all shadows by floating Burgundy on with water. When the shadows dry they will be anchored in place.

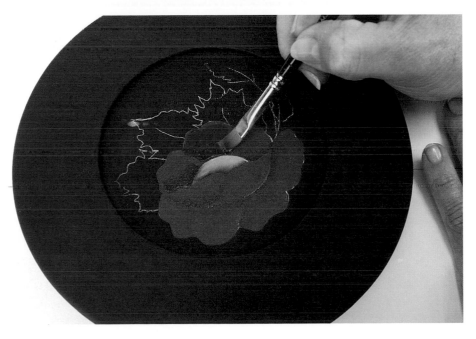

2. Paint one petal at a time. Begin with the back or most underneath petal and work toward the front. Apply painting and blending medium, but be careful not to get too much of it.

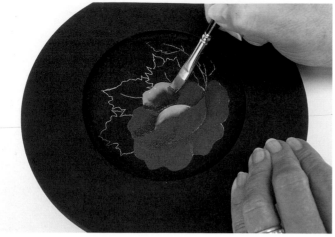

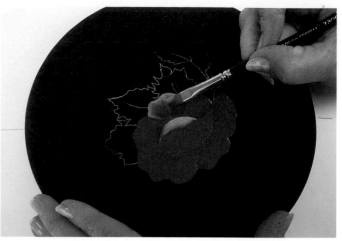

3. Apply *Cadmium Red Light*, *Cadmium Orange* and *Burgundy*, as shown on the worksheet. The Burgundy will create the shadows down the two sides and next to the center. Be sure you use plenty of paint. If you don't apply enough paint, you will not have enough color to blend and the paint will dry too quickly.

4. Using as large a flat brush as you are comfortable with, begin to pat the dark color up and the light color down, using a very light touch. If the paint is too thin, it will not want to properly blend. Add more paint, if needed. The blended strokes, which form the ripples and petal direction, almost resemble little tornadoes. Study these strokes on the worksheet.

After you have finished blending the first petal, paint the two side petals, then the three bottom petals, then the two front petals. The foremost front petal should be the lightest. Do notice the brushstroke direction.

5. To paint the poppy center, if needed, basecoat in white. Let dry and paint the center with *Hauser Green Light*. Anchor the *Burnt Umber* shadow. Let dry. Apply blending medium and *Hauser Green Light*. To shade, float on *Burnt Umber*. The tiny crater in the top of the poppy is created by double-loading a very small flat brush with *Hauser Green Light* and *Burnt Umber*. Blend on palette to soften the color, then paint a sideways U-stroke.

6. Double-load with *Hauser Green Light* and white. Blend to soften the color. Paint a sideways U-stroke opposite the first one.

𝒯ip

An easy, but effective poppy center can be created by dabbing on Burnt Umber, then highlighting with a touch of Ultramarine Blue that has been lightened with a little bit of white and Mauve. This center may be done in either oils or acrylics.

7. *Make the crater pop from the center by adding a comma stroke of Hauser Green Light and white placed under the dark edge.*

8. *A tiny comma of Hauser Green Light and Burnt Umber placed under the light edge will pop the light edge out.*

9. *To create the center sections, double-load your small flat brush with Hauser Green Light and Burnt Umber and pull the lines as shown on the worksheet. If desired you may highlight next to the Umber with a fine line of white.*

10. *The dots are painted with the point of the liner brush in Burnt Umber and white.*

Pattern for "Time for Flowers."

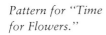

This pattern may be photocopied for personal use. Enlarge at 133 percent to return it to full size.

Poppy Worksheet in Oil

C.R.L.

B.A.

Pat blend poppy.

TURNED PETAL EDGE

Note stroke direction of the dark color.

THE WHITE POPPY

Titanium White

A mixture of Raw Umber, Mauve, Burnt Alizarin and Prussian Blue

THE CENTER

Dab on B.U.

Then dab on a touch of Ultramarine Blue and Mauve.

Poppy Worksheet in Acrylic

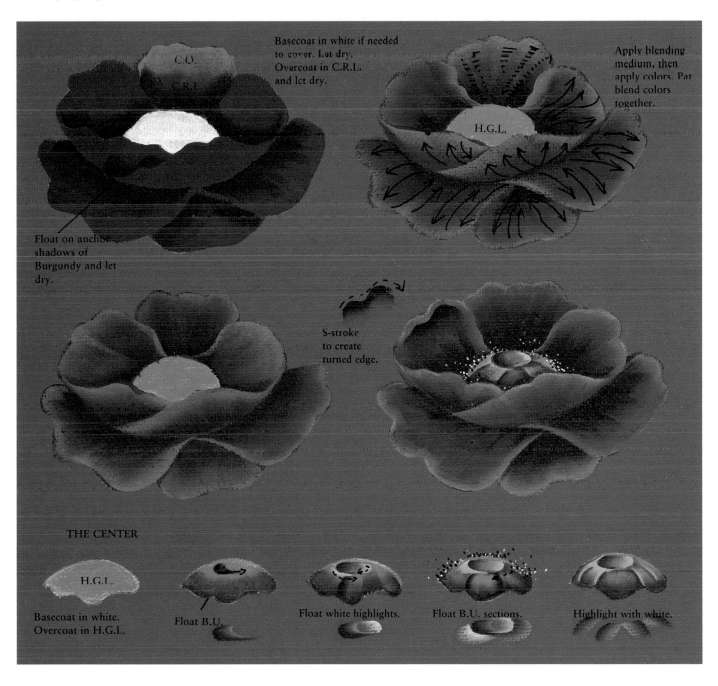

C.O.

C.R.L.

Basecoat in white if needed to cover. Let dry. Overcoat in C.R.L. and let dry.

Apply blending medium, then apply colors. Pat blend colors together.

H.G.L.

Float on anchor shadows of Burgundy and let dry.

S-stroke to create turned edge.

THE CENTER

H.G.L.

Basecoat in white. Overcoat in H.G.L.

Float B.U.

Float white highlights.

Float B.U. sections.

Highlight with white.

Pattern for end of footstool.

This pattern may be photocopied for personal use. Enlarge at 182 percent to return to full size.

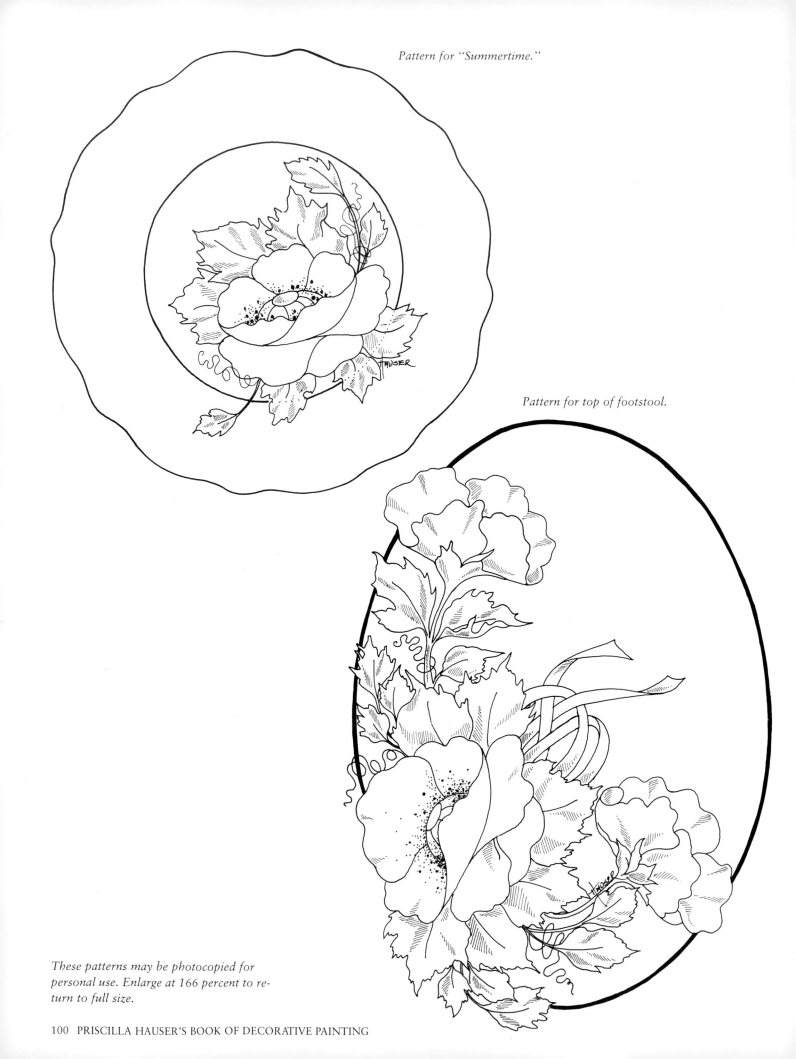

Pattern for "Summertime."

Pattern for top of footstool.

These patterns may be photocopied for personal use. Enlarge at 166 percent to return to full size.

"TIME FOR FLOWERS"
*A smoked surface with green trim creates
an exciting background for this Walnut
Hollow wooden clock. Instructions for the
smoking technique appear in chapter two.*

"A TOUCH OF RED AND YELLOW"
Stain this footstool in a rich warm brown.
Trim the center and the edges with black.

"SUMMERTIME"
This project demonstrates how attractive a
crackled finish can be. Basecoat the plate
in black and crackle the edge with Ice Blue.
The crackling technique is demonstrated
on this plate in chapter two.

Morning Glories

The grace and movement with which this flower and its leaves spread from the vine has always fascinated me, and its colors are simply wonderful. The demonstration is done with acrylics—remember, if using oils you can skip the basecoating and blending medium.

Colors Needed
Dioxazine Purple, Cerulean Blue, Prussian Blue, Titanium White, Hauser Green Light, Cadmium Yellow Light and Burnt Umber

Tip

To achieve the best results with acrylics:
- Use plenty of paint—you can't blend colors together unless you have enough wet paint to move one color into another.
- Use a large brush.
- Be sure your studio and paints are cold enough.

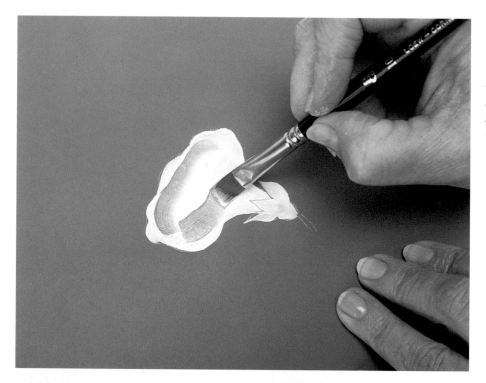

1. If you are using acrylics and painting on an extremely dark background, basecoat first in white. Let dry. Apply a little acrylic painting and blending medium and paint the inner edges Cerulean Blue.

2. Double-load the brush with Cerulean Blue and Dioxazine Purple, plus a touch of Prussian Blue, if desired. Blend on the palette to soften the color and shade the outside edges.

3. *Wipe the brush and double-load with white and Cerulean Blue. Apply the white to the center, blending it out into the Cerulean Blue. Fine lines of white may be added as shown on the worksheet.*

Study the worksheet where you will find the base of the flower is created by shading on Cerulean Blue, then shading with Dioxazine Purple. The center of the flower is created by blending a touch of Hauser Green Light out into the white. The egg-shaped portion is painted Cadmium Yellow Light. Next shade with a little Burnt Umber at the center and highlight the top with white. To paint the bud, basecoat in white. Let dry. Paint Cerulean Blue along the top edge and shade with Prussian Blue plus Dioxazine Purple.

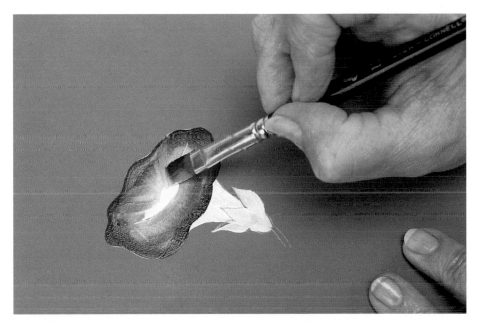

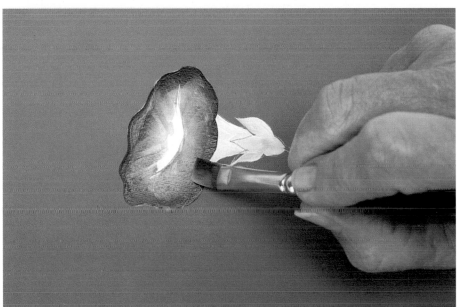

Morning Glory Worksheet

If using acrylics on a dark background, basecoat in white. Undercoat not necessary for oils.

Cerulean Blue

Dioxazine Purple plus a touch of Prussian Blue.

Double load with C.B. and D.P. Apply color around outside edge of flower.

Double-load with white and C.B. Apply white in center.

C.B.

D.P.

CENTER

H.G.L.

white

C.Y.L.

B.U.

A BUD

Basecoat in white if using acrylics.

Double-load with C.B. and D.P.

Pattern for front of watering can. This pattern may be photocopied for personal use.

Pattern for "Forever Spring."

*This pattern may be photocopied for personal use.
Enlarge at 147 percent and then again at 147 percent
to return it to full size.*

Pattern for "Say it With Flowers."

This pattern may be photocopied for personal use. Enlarge at 165 percent twice to return it to full size.

Pattern for neck of watering can.

Pattern for top of watering can.

These patterns may be photocopied for personal use. Enlarge at 160 percent to return to full size.

"SAY IT WITH FLOWERS"
Clean the metal mailbox thoroughly. Apply a good metal primer, then spray paint it off-white or the color of your choice before adding your decorative painting. Be sure to finish with an excellent outdoor finish.

"A LOVELY SUMMER SHOWER"
This watering can came from the hardware store. Clean it thoroughly with soap and water, then wipe with vinegar. Transfer the design and paint. Trim with bands of black.

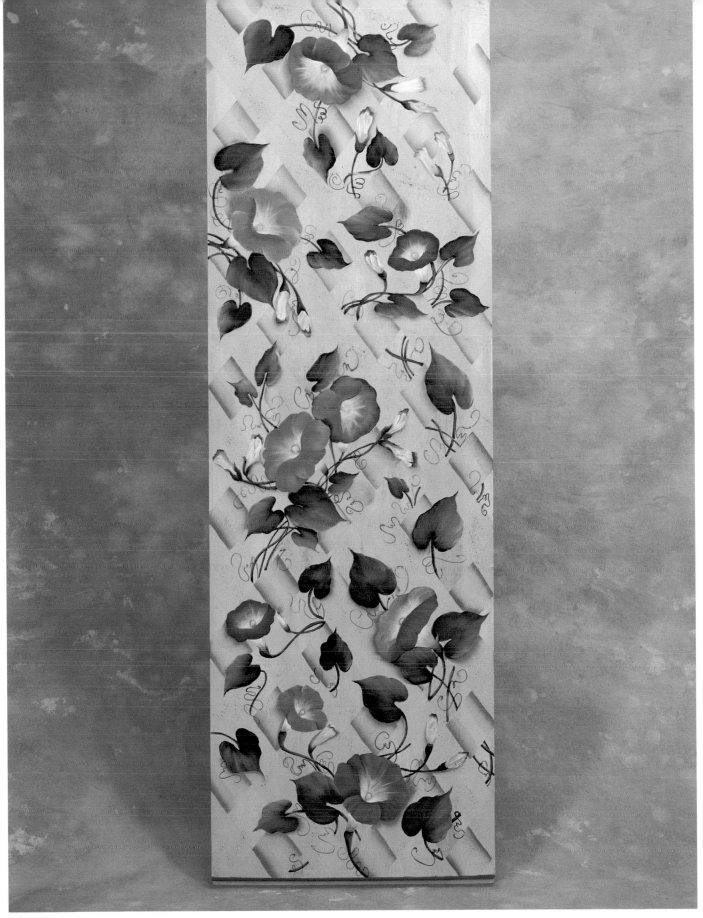

"FOREVER SPRING"
*Masking tape was used to paint the perfect
diagonals of the background trellis on this
old table leaf.*

Pansies

How can anyone resist a garden of pansies? These beautiful, velvety flowers have little faces that reflect the magic of God's touch. For this demonstration I have painted a yellow pansy using a freshly picked flower as a model. The worksheet will give you three other color possibilities. Pansies come in so many wonderful colors that I suggest studying a seed catalog, or better yet, a garden of these beautiful little flowers, for other color inspirations.

Colors Needed
- Yellow Pansy—Cadmium Yellow Medium, Burgundy, Prussian Blue, Titanium White, Cadmium Yellow Light, Hauser Green Light or Medium, and Cadmium Red
- Yellow and Purple Pansy—Burnt Carmine (if you can't find this color, use Burgundy mixed with a touch of Prussian Blue; substitute this mixture anywhere the following instructions call for Burnt Carmine), Cadmium Yellow Medium, Hauser Green Light, Burnt Umber, Titanium White and Cadmium Red Light
- Blue Pansy—Prussian Blue, mixture of Titanium White plus Prussian Blue
- Purple Pansy Bud—Dioxazine Purple and Titanium White

1. The brush size will depend upon the size of the flower you are painting. Basecoat the pansy in Cadmium Yellow Medium. Let dry.

My live pansy model.

2. Double-load the brush with water and the shadow color. Blend on the palette to soften the color and float to anchor the shadow. I used a mixture of Burgundy plus Prussian Blue. Let dry.

3. Anchor the shadow on the next petal.

4. Continue to anchor all the shadows.

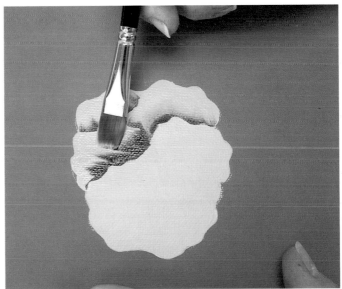

5. Apply painting and blending medium, Cadmium Yellow Medium and the shadow color. Start pat blending the dark color into the light, and the light color into the dark.

6. Apply painting and blending medium to the front petal. Then apply Cadmium Yellow Medium.

7. Double-load the brush with Cadmium Yellow Medium and shading color. Apply to the center of the pansy.

8. Begin to pat blend the color out into the petal, working from the center out. Follow the natural curve of the petal.

9. Continue blending the paint sideways, moving the dark out and the light in.

10. To paint the pansy center, use a fine liner brush and thin white. Centers must be neatly and carefully painted. Without a delicate center, the delicate feel of the flower can be lost. Paint two comma-like strokes that join all the petals. The tails open onto the edge of the lead petal.

11. Carefully paint the center of the pansy with Cadmium Yellow Light or Cadmium Yellow Medium.

12. Streak a little yellow out onto the dark shading on the lead petal.

13. Apply a little light or medium-value green in the center.

14. *Using a liner brush, add a tiny dot of Cadmium Red Light.*

15. *Shade under the green center with a little of the pansy shading color.*

Pat blending takes time and practice. Study the following tips to ensure your success.

1. Always pat blend with as large a brush as you can be comfortable with.

2. Use a very light touch.

3. You are actually blending the paint sideways: move dark colors into light and light colors into dark.

4. Be generous with the amount of paint you are using, and pick up more anytime you need it.

5. Blend following the natural direction or flow of the petal or object you are blending.

6. Be sure your room is cool and that no air is blowing on your paint.

7. If using oils, be sure you use thick-consistency paint and a light touch so you don't muddy or overblend the area. If this occurs, simply wipe the paint off and start again.

8. Have patience with yourself! This technique requires lots of practice to get it right.

THE YELLOW AND PURPLE PANSY

Double-load with a mix of white and B.C. and blend.

Burnt Carmine

Basecoat in white (for acrylics), then C.Y.M.

Float B.C.

Blend back with C.Y.M.

CENTER

H.G.L.

C.Y.M.

B.U.

B.C.

white

Note: Burgundy plus a touch of Prussian Blue may be substituted wherever Burnt Carmine is used.

Pansy Worksheet

THE BLUE PANSY

Double-load with mix of light blue and blend.

P.B. plus a touch of white

Basecoat in a mix of white plus P.B.

Float P.B.

Blend back with light blue.

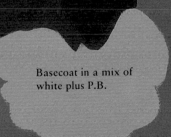

THE PURPLE BUD

D.P.

D.P. plus white

Blending on Raw Wood Worksheet

BASKET
1 Transfer pattern with graphite. Apply blending medium to raw wood. Apply white plus Burnt Umber (light brown mix).

2 Double-load with Burnt Umber and light brown mix. Apply shadows.

3 Apply Ice Blue highlights. Blend.

NEST AND GRASS

1 Apply medium. Apply thin Burnt Umber.

2 Shade with B.U.

EGGS

1 Apply white plus a touch of Burnt Umber and Prussian Blue.

3 Create texture on the straw nest with fine, wavy lines of B.U., Burnt Sienna, a light brown mixture, white or Ice Blue. Let the lines be loose and free. Apply the grass using a full liner brush of very thin Hauser Green Dark.

2 Shade with Burnt Umber and Prussian Blue or Payne's Gray.

3 Blend

4 Continue to texture the straw nest with fine linework. Apply thin Hauser Green Medium and Hauser Green Light to the grass. Accent with a few blades of Burnt Umber. Notice the grass starts at one point with the blades growing upward from that center point. A shadow may be applied under the nest if desired.

Pattern for "From My Garden With Love."

This pattern may be photocopied for personal use. Enlarge at 118 percent to return it to full size.

Pattern for front of saltbox.

These patterns may be photocopied for personal use.

Pattern for top of saltbox.

PANSIES

Pattern for lid of saltbox.

Pattern for "Frame it With Flowers."

"PANSIES AND PLAID"
*This salt or tea box takes on new interest
when painted with lively plaids. Create a
plaid to match your decor using fabric or
ribbon for color ideas.*

"FRAME IT WITH FLOWERS"

This wooden frame by Walnut Hollow was first painted a light brown color. I then applied Burnt Umber over the light brown using a technique similar to sponging, but instead of using a sponge, I used a piece of plastic wrap that I crushed together in my hand. The edges are trimmed in green.

"FROM MY GARDEN WITH LOVE"
This beautiful raw wood plank is available
from Walnut Hollow. To prepare it, sand
the surface and wipe with a tack rag. Transfer the design and then paint according to
directions for blending on raw wood given
in chapter three and on the raw wood
worksheet.

Irises

The different colors of irises are simply incredible. When you paint this beautiful flower for the first time, try to imagine that each petal is constructed much like a leaf. Both irises and tulips lend themselves beautifully to a vertical format.

This demonstration is painted in acrylics. If using oils, generally the undercoating and the anchor are not necessary. Simply apply the colors, beginning with the back or most underneath petal and work forward, blending each petal neatly and carefully using a very light touch. Always be sure your paint is the proper consistency for the technique you are using. Regardless of whether you are using acrylics or oils for dry-brush blending, the paint should be a thick consistency.

Colors Needed
Titanium White, Dioxazine Purple, Prussian Blue, Cadmium Yellow Light and Cadmium Yellow Medium

1. The size of the flat brushes you use will depend on the size of the design you're painting. You'll also need an excellent no. 1 liner or scroll brush. If painting with acrylics on a dark background, I recommend basecoating neatly and smoothly in white. Let dry and reapply the pattern, if needed. Anchor the shadows by floating on Dioxazine Purple. Let dry. Anytime you are dry-brush blending with acrylics, it is always good to float an anchor.

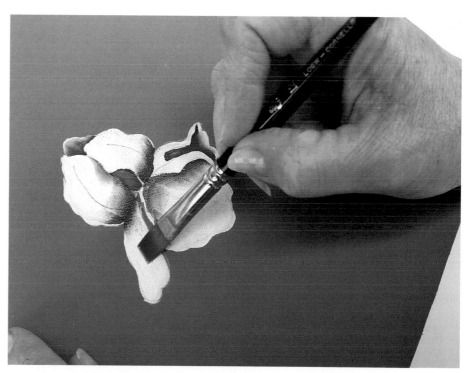

2. Begin painting one petal at a time starting at the back and working forward. If using acrylics, first apply painting and blending medium to the petal you are working on.

3. *Make a mixture of light purple using Titanium White plus a touch of Dioxazine Purple and Prussian Blue. Apply white to the outside edge of the petal and then apply the light purple mixture. Double-load the brush with the light purple mixture and the shading color. Blend on palette to soften the color. Apply the shadows, as shown on the worksheet.*

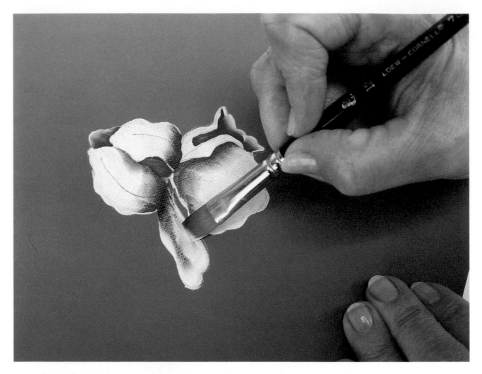

4. *Wipe the brush and gently pat and blend the petals following the natural curve or direction each petal flows from the center outward.*

5. *Located in the center of the petals is the "beard." To create the beard on the iris I have used tiny dots of Cadmium Yellow Medium, Cadmium Yellow Light and white.*

Iris Worksheet

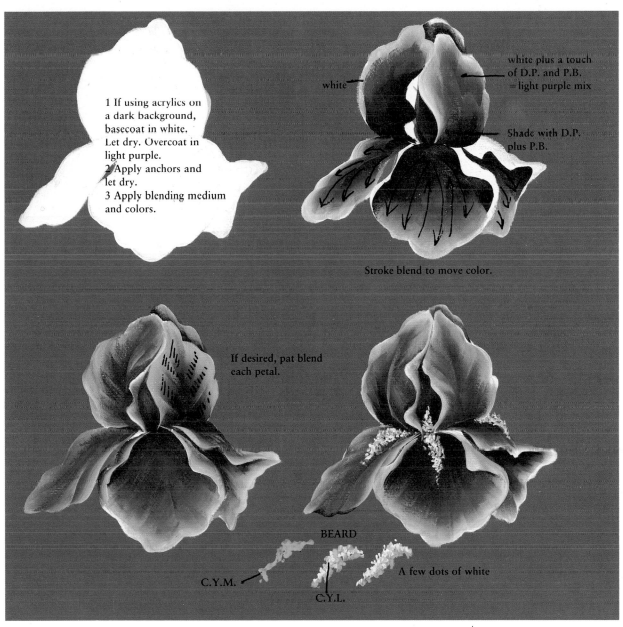

1 If using acrylics on a dark background, basecoat in white. Let dry. Overcoat in light purple.
2 Apply anchors and let dry.
3 Apply blending medium and colors.

white

white plus a touch of D.P. and P.B. = light purple mix

Shade with D.P. plus P.B.

Stroke blend to move color.

If desired, pat blend each petal.

BEARD

C.Y.M.

C.Y.L.

A few dots of white

Pattern for "Sunshine Blossoms."

This pattern may be photocopied for personal use. Enlarge at 143 percent to return it to full size.

"SUNSHINE BLOSSOMS"
It really makes you feel good when you've
created a piece for your home. This lamp
base is available from Walnut Hollow.
Lamp kits—which include all the necessary
wiring and hardware—can be purchased at
craft and decorating stores to turn this
wooden base into a functional lamp.

Magnolias and Other Blossom Flowers

The magnolia, the elegant gardenia and many of our blossom-type flowers can all be painted in a similar manner. The most important part of creating these beautiful flowers is to be certain your brushstrokes are flowing with the movement and the direction of each petal. Study these flowers carefully as God has created them to understand the direction and movement of the petals.

Colors Needed

Magnolia—Titanium White, Cadmium Yellow Light, Burnt Umber, Burnt Sienna, Raw Sienna, Hauser Green Light and Hauser Green Dark

1. The size of the flat brush you will use depends upon the size of the design you are painting. Remember, when blending always work with as large a brush as you can possibly be comfortable with. You will also need a no. 1 liner or scroll brush. If using acrylics and painting on a dark background, basecoat neatly and carefully in white. Let dry and retransfer the design, if necessary.

2. Basecoat the center with Cadmium Yellow Light. Apply Burnt Umber to the base of the center. If using acrylics, anchor the shadows. If painting with oils, this step is not necessary.

3. On the worksheet, I shaded the back petals with Raw Sienna. Let dry.

4. Apply painting and blending medium to one petal at a time. Double-load the brush with white and the shading color. I used a mixture of Burnt Umber plus a touch of Hauser Green Dark. When these colors are mixed together, you get an almost silvery-gray color. Apply the paint as shown on the worksheet. Wipe the brush and blend. More paint and shadow color may be added, as needed. The flowers can be as light or dark as you desire.

5. Paint the center Cadmium Yellow Light and shade at the base with Burnt Umber. Double-load the brush with Yellow and Burnt Sienna and shade again, as shown on the worksheet. Double-load the brush with Yellow and Hauser Green Light and apply the highlight at the top of the center as shown. Wipe the brush and double-load with the dirty brush and white. Begin painting tiny U-type strokes at the top of the center, building down toward the bottom.

The Tulip Blossom

The Tulip Blossom shown on the tulip worksheet, page 138, is created the same way. The shading color is Raw Sienna and Burgundy or Burnt Alizarin. A touch of Burnt Umber may be added to the Burgundy for additional depth, if desired.

Pattern for "Southern Elegance."
This pattern may be photocopied for personal use. Enlarge at 200 percent to return to original size.

Magnolia Worksheet

white

R.S.

B.U. plus H.G.D.

C.Y.L.

B.U.

If using acrylics basecoat in white.
Anchor R.S. shadows.

2

4

3

H.G.L.

6

R.S.

B.S.

7

5

1

white U-strokes

B.U. and H.G.D.

white

Apply colors and blend one petal at a time.
Start at the back and work forward.

Blend.

Pattern for top of trinket box.

These patterns may be photocopied for personal use. Enlarge at 154 percent to return to full size.

Pattern for back of hand mirror.

"SOUTHERN ELEGANCE"
This lovely wooden Walnut Hollow tray was basecoated in black. Its rim was painted with Hauser Green Dark, then sponged with black. Step-by-step sponging techniques for this tray are shown in chapter two.

"THROUGH MY LOOKING GLASS"
I purchased these pieces already covered with fabric, but you can cover your own inexpensive box and plastic mirror with fabric, stuffed with synthetic stuffing. Use hot glue to hold the fabric in place, then glue trim over the edges. Transfer the magnolia pattern and paint.

Tulips

Spring would not be spring without tulips. On the worksheet, I have created a broken tulip. These are tulips with a streaked effect, created by breaking the background color with delicate pat blending strokes of another color. These tulips were particularly loved by the Dutch in the seventeenth century. Their colors can vary. Tulips lend themselves beautifully to a vertical format.

Colors Needed
- Yellow Tulip—Titanium White, Burnt Sienna, Cadmium Yellow Medium, Burnt Umber and Hauser Green Medium
- Broken Tulip—Titanium White, Burnt Alizarin or Burgundy, Prussian Blue, Hauser Green Medium and Burnt Umber
- Tulip Blossom—Titanium White, Raw Sienna, Burnt Alizarin or Burgundy, Cadmium Yellow Light, Hauser Green Light, Burnt Sienna and Burnt Umber

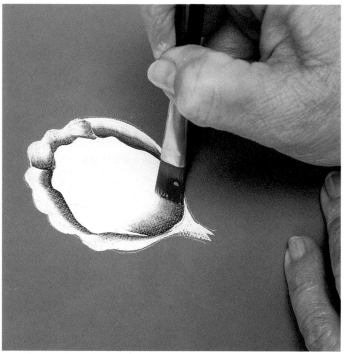

1. The size of the brush you use depends upon the size of the tulip you are painting. I used my flat brushes and a no. 1 liner or scroll brush. Undercoat with white if painting with acrylics. Let dry. Double-load the flat brush with water and Burnt Sienna. Anchor the shadows.

2. Begin with the back petal. Apply painting and blending medium to the petal. Then double-load the brush with Cadmium Yellow Medium and Burnt Sienna. Apply the color to the tulip.

3. Apply painting and blending medium, white, Cadmium Yellow Medium and Burnt Sienna. Use a large brush and blend.

4. Begin stroke blending by stroking from the bottom to the top and from the top to the bottom.

5. Begin pat blending by pulling the Burnt Sienna into the paint sideways creating little tornadoes. This creates movement within the petals.

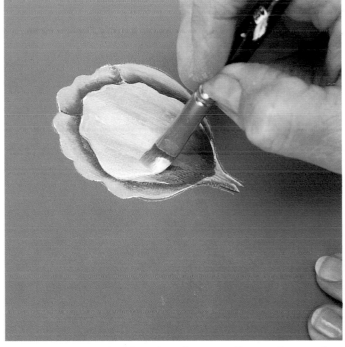

6. Double-load the brush with Cadmium Yellow Medium and white, and paint an S-type stroke to accent the edge of the petal. This may be done at random, but don't overdo it. Paint the stems green. Shade with a little Burnt Umber and highlight with a little white.

Broken Tulip Worksheet

1 If using acrylics, basecoat in white and let dry. Reapply pattern.
2 Anchor shadows.
3 Apply blending medium.
4 Work one petal at a time.

H.G.M.

white

white

B.A. or Burgundy

Apply colors to back petals and blend.

white

white

B.A.

B.A. or Burgundy plus P.B.

Don't be afraid to "play" with this! Each one turns out a little differently.

Double-load and overstroke petals.

B.U.

white blending

stroking

THE TULIP BLOSSOM

1 6 2

5 white

8 7

3 white 4 R.S. shading (just a touch)

1 If using acrylics, basecoat with white and let dry. Reapply pattern.
2 Anchor shadows.
3 Apply blending medium.
4 Work one petal at a time.

CENTER

white

C.Y.L. B.S.

H.G.L. B.U.

white

R.S. plus B.A. or Burgundy

Apply colors.

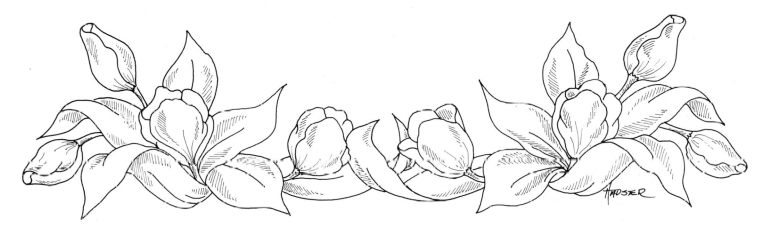

Pattern for front of tin basket. This pattern may be photocopied for personal use. Enlarge at 167 percent to return it to full size.

Pattern for end of tin basket. This pattern may be photocopied for personal use. Enlarge at 133 percent to return it to full size.

Pattern for "A Gathering of Spring." This pattern may be photocopied for personal use. Enlarge at 222 percent (or enlarge 149 percent twice) to return it to full size.

"A GATHERING OF SPRING"
This raw tin piece was purchased at a garden store. Wash with soap and water and wipe with vinegar. Transfer the tulip pattern and paint.

"A YELLOW SPRING FLING"
This raw tin basket was prepared in the
same way as the tin vase. Tin pieces like
this can be found at garden stores, home
decorating and specialty import shops, and
in some of the larger craft stores.

Index